A Reflective Question to Ponder

1,200+ Questions on Autism to Foster Dialogue

Scott R. Frasard, PhD

First published 2024
by Dr. Scott R. Frasard

© 2024 Dr. Scott R. Frasard

The right of Scott R. Frasard to be identified as the author of this work has been asserted to him in accordance with sections 77 and 78 of the Copyright, Designs and Patents Act of 1988.

All rights reserved. No part of this book may be reprinted or reproduced or utilized in any form or by any electronic, mechanical, or other means, now known or hereafter invented, including photocopying and recording, or in any information storage or retrieval system, without permission in writing form the publishers.

Trademark notice: Product or corporate names may be trademarks or registered trademarks, and are used only for identification and explanation without intent to infringe.

Library of Congress Cataloging-in Publication Data
A catalog record for this title has been requested

ISBN: 979-8-9884823-0-7

Typeset in Palatino Linotype

Dedication

To my incredible autistic community:

    With all my heart, I dedicate this book to you. It is through your strength, wisdom, and unwavering support that I have found my voice, my purpose, and my place in this world. You welcomed me into your world with open arms, and in doing so, you changed my life forever.

    Learning that I'm autistic at the age of 48 was like discovering a hidden part of myself that had been waiting for me all along. The journey that followed was one of self-discovery, acceptance, and profound growth. But I did not walk this path alone. You were there with me every step of the way, offering insights that challenged my perceptions, stories that resonated deeply within me, and a sense of belonging that I had never known before.

    Your perspectives opened my eyes to the richness of our shared experiences and the beauty of our neurodiversity. You showed me that being autistic is not something to be fixed or hidden but something to be celebrated and embraced. You taught me that our differences are our strengths and that our voices, when united, can bring about powerful change.

    This book is more than just a collection of questions and reflections; it is a testament to the incredible impact you have had on my life and the lives of so many others. It is a tribute to your resilience, your creativity, and your unwavering commitment to advocating for a world where autistic people are understood, respected, and valued for who we are.

Thank you for being my teachers, my friends, my inspirations. Thank you for challenging me to think differently, to question deeply, and to advocate passionately. Thank you for showing me that I am not alone, and for giving me the courage to stand up and speak out.

This book is for you, and because of you. I am forever grateful for your support, your encouragement, and your love. Together, we are more than just a community; we are a movement, a force for change, and a beacon of hope.

With all my love and deepest gratitude,

Scott Frasard

CONTENTS

Forward	i
Acknowledgements	v
Introduction	vii
Chapter 1: My Autistic Journey	1
Chapter 2: Framing Autism	15
Questions 1 – 301	19
Chapter 2 Wrap-Up	67
Chapter 3: Talking about autism	69
Questions 302 – 560	72
Chapter 3 Wrap-Up	112
Chapter 4: Autism and people	113
Questions 561 – 684	115
Chapter 4 Wrap-Up	134
Chapter 5: Social Interactions	135
Questions 685 – 820	141
Chapter 5 Wrap-Up	162
Chapter 6: Autism, Support, and Services	163
Questions 821 – 1,052	165
Chapter 6 Wrap-Up	200

Chapter 7: Autism Advocacy	201
Questions 1,053 – 1,226	204
Chapter 7 Wrap-Up	232
Chapter 8: All Perspectives are Valid	233
Chapter 9: A Relational Model to Understand Neurodiversity	241
Chapter 10: Rethinking Support, Disability, and Advocacy	253
Afterward	263
The Autistic Bill of Rights	267
About the Author	271

Forward

Our life is directed by the quality of the questions we ask. When the intention behind your questions comes from compassionate curiosity with the goal to learn more about yourself and others in connection and community, you are elevating growth and humanity. This foundation of compassionate curiosity to foster connection is the basis for the Mind Your Autistic Brain #ShineALight Autistic Advocate campaign and it has been my honor and privilege to invite Scott Frasard to be a part of this annual campaign since 2022. Scott and I had our first "April Autism Awareness Month" wrap up conversation in 2022 where we discussed exactly what you will be learning and reading more about in this powerful book—how to foster connection and change through quality questions.

The reason *A Reflective Question to Ponder* is such an important and revolutionary approach is because it is the unanswered questions, the unasked questions, and the questions that lead to conflict rather than fruitful dialogue, which create the broken narrative that currently permeates what autism truly is from those who are actually autistic. It is this misunderstanding that drains our energy, exhausts our resources, overwhelms our thoughts and sensory systems, and leads to chronic cycle burnout. When others view you in ways that are not accurate or in alignment with who you know yourself to be, that wide gap leads to burnout.

Discovering you are autistic as an adult is a complex experience which includes the emotions of relief, elation, validation, regret, frustration, shame, fear, and more often than not an identity crisis. Most late identified adults learn they are autistic after suffering the worst burnout of their life. The experience of living your entire life feeling and knowing you are different from others, yet not having any explanation for it, leaves many of us exhausted. The exhaustion is commonly attributed to masking and/or camouflaging, sensory sensitivities, and high-speed brains that get caught in thought loops trying to understand and navigate the world around us and so much more. Scott has assembled an array of questions on some of the hottest topics in the autistic community here in this book that will #FlipTheAutisticScript and open conversation, which allows for connection, viewing of differing perspectives, and overall change in how the world views autism and how we as autistics view ourselves.

Understanding ourselves and others is where so much of our energy and attention goes as autistics. In this powerful and transformational dive into what autism means from a spectrum of quality questions and individuals my good friend, NeuroDrive Team colleague, and all-around fabulous human and advocate, Scott Frasard, will break through unconscious bias in ways you never imagined. You will be cheering along as you have personal breakthrough moments and revelations of self, question by question.

I have been truly gifted by Scott's friendship over the last few years. My brain and heart are continually sparked full of joy every time we visit. Scott Frasard is one of the true genius minds of our time and his compassion and curiosity make him one of the best researchers and community builders today. The opportunity to see into his brilliance and to also be transformed in spectacular ways is what this book will do for you, at the very least.

"What assumptions are made about autistic people?" "What assumptions are made about neuromajority people?" We often begin with what we believe and those beliefs influence how we communicate with others, how we behave towards others, and how we view ourselves. If you are ready to explore a variety of quality questions that will get you thinking in ways you never imagined possible and to have fun as you explore what autism is and can be, hop into chapter one. Don't miss out on

Scott's invitation to share and experiment with the questions he shares in this book for yourself.

Carole Jean Whittington

Burnout Restoration Strategist
Mind Your Autistic Brain, Founder
Mind Your Autistic Brain Talk Show, Host
The Brian Dump Blog
The UnVeiling Method
The Neurodiverse Communication EcoSystem
Her Brain Connection Lab
Author of, "How Spicy is Your Burnout?"
www.MindYourAutisticBrain.com
www.Resources.MindYourAutisticBrain.com

Acknowledgements

I respectfully acknowledge and honor the original stewards of the lands on which I've had the privilege to reside. The Tribal Nations' profound connection to these lands and their enduring legacy of care and respect are deeply inspiring and deserving of our gratitude. These Tribal Nations include:

- Coahuiltecan
- Goshute
- Hinono'eino' biito'owu' (Arapaho)
- Ishak (Atakapa)
- Jumanos
- Karankawa
- Mvskoke (Muscogee)
- Ndé Kónitsąąíí Gokíyaa (Lipan Apache)
- Newe Sogbia (Eastern Shoshone)
- Nʉmʉnʉʉ Sookobitʉ (Comanche)
- Núu-agha-tʉvʉ-pʉ̱ (Ute)
- Očhéthi Šakówiŋ
- Pueblos
- Tigua (Tiwa)
- Timpanogos
- ᏣᎳᎫᏪᏘᏱ Tsalaguwetiyi (Cherokee, East)
- Tséstho'e (Cheyenne)
- Tonkawa
- Piro
- Sana
- S'atsoyaha (Yuchi)

Introduction

"I think a question has the only capacity to be flexible enough to be wisdom."

~ Hannah Gadsby

If you're reading this, I want to thank you. This book is a product of a year-long experiment in advocating for myself as an autistic person and, by extension, advocating for the autistic community at-large. The reflective questions in this book will challenge you to think deeply, reflect critically, and examine your own beliefs and assumptions. They will stir a range of emotions—making you angry at injustices, gasp at revelations, and wonder why some questions haven't been asked before. You may find solace in seeing your silent questions finally spoken; you may feel outrage at other questions daring to be voiced. The journey through the book will be one of introspection and empathy, encouraging you to engage with perspectives you may not have considered, including your own.

I didn't set out to be an advocate. My path into advocacy began with a simple desire to share my experiences as someone identified as autistic later in life. Reflecting on my autistic journey, both before and after identification, I embraced social media as both an outlet and a place for connection. I also began paying attention to the voices of established autistic advocates. In a short time, my own sharing repertoire turned more advocate-like.

Soon, I was making proclamations of what others needed to know about autism and autistic people. I began to resemble a parrot, repeating in my own voice the messages of select autistic advocates. It didn't take long to feel that something was missing. Much like a parrot's repeated phrases often go unnoticed, the one-way communication that so often happens on social media fell short in fostering meaningful change. Among the vocal advocates, individuals were not taking the time to listen, only to speak.

Getting people to talk about their differing perspectives is the first, and most critical, step in bringing about meaningful, sustainable change. When people can share their perspectives honestly, without ridicule, something very important happens—trust is built, which sets the stage for them to listen. One of the best ways to accomplish meaningful change to improve autistics' lives is by opening ourselves up and listening to others first. There is a limit to how much people are willing to hear before shutting down the communication process and stop being receptive to any messages. To me, the missing ingredient in the autism advocacy strategy was true dialogue rather than mere discussion. In dialogue, participants set aside their perspectives, freely explore others' perspectives, and engage in deep listening to understand why others hold their perspectives. This allows each person to reflect on their own world views in light of others' perspectives in a search for their "truth." Discussion, on the other hand, is more aligned with a debate, where people attempt to convince others that their perspective is the truth and should be adopted.

After seeing so many advocates comment about "infighting" within the autistic community, I decided that a different (perhaps "new") approach to autism advocacy was needed. People from all perspectives on the big issues where the autistic community demanded change needed to listen to one another so the right issues are addressed the right way at the right time. Something needed to reduce the emotions that typically run high during discussions on topics as sensitive as applied behavior analysis and finding a cure for autism in favor of something logical so solutions could be found. There was a need for dialogue, but how? The answer: ask questions!

Socrates[1] believed that asking questions enables us to examine ideas logically and to determine if those ideas were valid. By asking questions, we gain clarification, understand what's really being asked, explore reason and evidence, gain insights into the origin of the issue, see the implications and consequences, and to truly see others' perspectives. In doing so, no one perspective is promoted as being the "truth" while allowing people to critically reflect on their worldviews to develop the fullest possible knowledge set about any given topic. Socratic questioning is intimately connected to critical thinking,[2] which is what's needed to unify the autistic community for a better future for all autistic people. It was my "ah-ha" moment—use questions to do the following relative to autism[3]:

- Raise basic issues
- Probe beneath the surface of things
- Pursue problematic areas of thought
- Discover the thought structure of others
- Develop sensitivity to clarity, accuracy, relevance, and depth
- Arrive at judgments through reasoning
- Analyze thinking—its purposes, assumptions, questions, points of view, information, inferences, concepts, and implications

So, I set off with my new brand of advocacy. Using LinkedIn, one of my primary social media platforms for sharing my ideas, where I had a sizeable following, I posted this message in late March 2022 to get things going:

> April is an interesting month for the autistic community. There are people who seek to raise our consciousness about autism through

---

[1] Socrates was a Greek philosopher who challenged conventional wisdom and inspired many followers, including Plato and Aristotle.
[2] Paul, R., & Elder, L. (2016). *The thinker's guide to Socratic questioning.* Foundation for Critical Thinking Press.
[3] Paul & Elder 2016, p. 5

various perspectives and organizations that seek to raise money to help in a variety of ways.

April is also a time of contention between and among different groups and individuals that make up this wonderful community. The variety of perspectives provides us a wealth of knowledge and insights into autism's complexity.

Having a voice in the chaos is challenging at best and can feel futile at worst. From my vantage point, I observe people and organizations alike sharing information and placing a stake in the ground on their truth. We live in an amazing time where we can do this and have our views heard by millions of people across the globe.

One of the things I love about the autistic community is that we are different from the majority of the world's population. Within our community we have a wide range of expressions, which creates a vibrant fabric of human experience. Another thing I love about this community is that we get to share these experiences so others can sample what our world is like in the hopes that our differences are minimized and commonalities maximized.

At times our voices are a cacophony of noises and discontent while other times they are a harmonious symphony of love and respect. I like to think both serve a purpose—to move us to be better humans. Everyone gains as much from perspective differences as we do from common bonds. It's difficult to not be upset when our perspectives are denigrated with a similar strength as we feel a kinship when our views fit together like a dovetail joint.

I am autistic. I am a self-advocate. I have strongly held perspectives that I have refined over the years. I share these perspectives. Many other autistics on this platform[4] share the same, or similar, perspectives while others do not. Some share my perspectives among their network, which I love, while others dismantle, which I try to not take personally. There is a lot of give and take in any sort of social justice movement, which is what I see still in action from at least the 1990's with Judy Singer's[5] seminal work that gave us the term "neurodiversity."

I've planted my stake in the ground when it comes to certain things about autism, autism as an identity, and autism as a human experience. I am proud to be autistic and for me, the perspectives I hold are my truth. I've also made it a point to foster true dialogue within and without the autistic community to better understand those who have different perspectives. I ask reflective questions here, and in real life, to spur a thoughtful exchange of ideas.

If you've read this far—thank you. I sincerely appreciate your time. As we push forward, let's remember why we care so much and be respectful of others' views.

#FlipTheAutisticScript
#AutismUnderstanding
#ActuallyAutistic
#ThisIsWhatAutismLooksLike

In the nine months that followed, I posted almost daily about topics and issues that came to mind as a natural course of curiosity as well as topics others brought up on various social media platforms. In total, I posted:

---

[4] LinkedIn
[5] Judy Singer's original master's thesis was published in 1998, which gave rise to the term "neurodiversity." This work was later turned into the book, *Neurodiversity: The birth of an idea*.

- 1,448 questions
- 261 polls
- 375 posts

The questions spanned about 50 different topics, which I loosely categorized into six broad domains. The countless responses provided much insight into the differing perspectives and helped me refine my own perspectives. There was the occasional malcontent posted, but they were redirected to a more productive dialogue. I witnessed what I felt was needed – the coming together of different minds to talk about the things that needed to be talked about for everyone's benefit, but especially for the autistic person's benefit. Because of my positive experience, I decided to take my questions I posed and create this book to serve as a guide and reference for others to use. I believe that anyone can replicate this approach and foster a fruitful dialogue.

Book Organization and How to Use

This book is organized into 10 chapters. The first chapter traces my autistic journey from being formally identified as autistic to my transition to an autistic autism advocate, which provides context for the questions. Chapters two through seven contain the actual questions I posted throughout 2022. These questions delve into various aspects of autism, including framing autism (Chapter 2), talking about autism (Chapter 3), autism and people (Chapter 4), social interactions (Chapter 5), autism, support, and services (Chapter 6), and autism advocacy (Chapter 7).

The concluding trio of chapters are my original works, tackling what I perceive as being three overarching issues that the autistic community faces. This begins with Chapter 8 exploring the matter that all perspectives are valid, which is a central premise to my advocacy approach. In Chapter 9, I introduce an alternative perspective on neurodiversity through a relational model. Here, I peel back the layers of assumptions found in the current social constructs on neurodiversity. I am, instead, to highlight what truly connects us as humans navigating the world: our shared experiences. Finally, in Chapter 10, I propose transformative actions to help reframe our understanding of support, disability, and advocacy.

This book can be read from start to finish, or you can jump back and forth through the chapters as you ponder the aspects of autism important to you and the autistic community. It offers the chance to explore 1,200+ thought-provoking questions about autism, autistic culture, and society's constructs of both. Whether you choose to read it cover to cover or skip around to the chapters that intrigue you the most, you're invited to reflect on your own perspectives and ask others for theirs. Embrace the opportunity to engage with this book, and I'm confident it will inspire you to see autism in a new light.

As you delve into these questions, consider engaging in verbal dialogue with others or sharing questions from the book on your social media platforms. You are welcome to leverage the questions from this book either verbatim or rephrase any in a way that works better for you. Additionally, if you teach, regardless of the context, please consider using these questions in your classroom to foster dialogue about autism relative to your subject or setting. By drawing questions from these pages, you can spark enlightening conversations that enhance understanding, break down barriers and stigmas, and become a positive voice for or within the autistic community.

In whatever ways you decide to use this book, I hope you enjoy it and that it will cause you to pause to reflect on your perspectives, as well as others' perspectives. This will be helpful for all beyond measure!

Thank you!
Scott

Chapter 1
My Autistic Journey

"I am no longer afraid of becoming lost, because the journey back always reveals something new, and that is ultimately good for the artist."

~ Billy Joel

How it Started

My autistic journey began in 2019 when I was 47. My wife and I were watching a new docuseries on the A&E Network called *The Employables*[6]. I was immediately smitten by the show and every time they showed an autistic person, I felt a deep, yet unexplainable connection to their plight.

At first, my wife and I made casual comments about how I had similar experiences as the autistic people on the show. We'd point out the things I did like them, such as stimming or being too shy to make my own cold calls. Initially, though, I didn't think much of it beyond coincidence. Then, after having watched three or four episodes, I started to wonder, "What if... *I am autistic?*" I kept this thought from my wife because I didn't want to be seen as dramatic, overreacting, or looking for excuses for my lived experiences. After all, I was married, had lived

---

[6] "The Employables" follows neurodivergent job seekers as they work to overcome obstacles and find fulfilling employment that provides them with the skills to excel long term in their careers. Each episode charts the highs and lows of two job seekers in their hunt for work. To help achieve their dreams, each participant works with an autism or Tourette Syndrome specialist to identify their strengths and determine how best to pursue their job search. With new tools at hand, each job seeker sets out on interviews or trial runs with potential employers to find the perfect line of work. For more information, go to: https://www.aetv.com/shows/the-employables

independently for about 30 years, traveled the globe as a very successful professional, was recognized as an expert in my field, and had earned multiple advanced degrees – certainly I couldn't be… autistic! I experienced mixed feelings of genuine curiosity, as I related so much to the autistic people I watched on the show, and disbelief. What I thought I knew about autism as a medical professional[7] gave me the belief that I would not have experienced so much success in my life if I were autistic! And yet, there, on the screen, I could see my lived experiences reflected at me through the lives of others.

Around the fourth episode, I started looking up free online tests to satiate my curiosity. I eventually found the Aspie-Quiz[8], which checks for atypical (autistic) and typical (neurotypical) traits in adults and provides a potential indication of autism prior to a formal identification. I took the quiz one day while we watched the newest episode of *The Employables*. Although I don't remember my exact score, I do recall that it was above the threshold for suspected autism. I reflected on this result for a while as my wife and I continued to watch the show. At the next commercial break, I shared with my wife that I had taken the test and told her the results; she was not surprised. I shared the quiz link with her and she took the test as if she were me (she knows me VERY well—often better than I know myself!). We compared our results, and her score for me was higher than my score for myself. We had a brief conversation about the possibility of being autistic and that's when I started shifting from "What if I'm autistic?" to "I really could be autistic." I needed to find out.

After that day, time passed, but I couldn't stop thinking about the possibility of being autistic. I started reading about autism, the criteria for diagnosis, and how to be evaluated. I bought a few books on autism and read voraciously. The more I read, the clearer things became in my mind—I am definitely autistic! At this point, I didn't realize that self-identification is perfectly acceptable in the autistic

---

[7] I was a Paramedic for 22 years.
[8] http://www.rdos.net/eng/Aspie-quiz.php

community. I felt the need to find out for sure, with formal identification. I needed to have a name for why I had felt so different from the rest of the world my entire life. I had a feeling that doing so would give me control and direction—a way of making sense of what had been so confusing for me my entire life.

Searching for an Answer

I told my wife that I wanted an autism evaluation. She was very supportive but left it to me to find someone to conduct the evaluation. I started looking for psychologists in my area who specialized in evaluating adults for autism. I stumbled upon Psychology Today's website[9], which allowed me to search for a psychologist (in the United States) by using filters to refine my search via multiple criteria. Once I narrowed the possibilities, I could read a detailed narrative from each psychologist, see their picture, explore their background, and even send them an email through the website to get the conversation started. This last part was critical in obtaining a diagnosis, as I really do not like making cold calls and appointments.

As I found potential psychologists that I felt I could be comfortable with regarding evaluation and talking with me about autism, I sent out emails. And then I waited for replies. Not all replied, and many of the replies I did receive were to let me know they did not evaluate *adults* or they were not accepting new clients currently. I started to feel discouraged. I continued to search and email…and search and email. Eventually, I got a reply from one psychologist who was interested in evaluating me. We set up a time to chat on the phone to explore the possibility further. When we talked, I felt very comfortable with her and we agreed to move forward with an evaluation. I was actually going to be evaluated for autism, but my excitement was short-lived. She emailed me back later that day to let me know they

---

[9] https://www.psychologytoday.com/us/therapists

would not be able to do the evaluation, as her organization did not have the proper measurement instruments for evaluating adults.

After the cyclical excitement and let-down of a possible evaluation, I started feeling discouraged. I felt that formally confirming if I was autistic would give me answers to many mysteries in my life, but achieving a diagnosis seemed an impossibility. I continued my search for a suitable psychologist, but the options were getting fewer in number and further away from my location. Several rejection emails filled my inbox before I got another interested psychologist. This time, I did not get my hopes up and it was some time before I replied. I eventually I spoke with Dr. Amy Brown of Sound Mind Psychology in Austin, TX[10]. We spoke about my experiences, why I thought I might be autistic, and why I sought a diagnosis. We both felt comfortable and agreed to move forward with an evaluation. After some back and forth between her office and my insurance company, an initial meeting was set. It was really going to happen!

I actually had some mixed emotions about being evaluated and possibly identified as autistic. I had so many questions going through my head: What would the evaluation entail? How long will it take? Will it bring up negative emotions? Will I need to include my mother to provide insights of me as a child? Will I need to include my wife to provide insights of me as an adult other than my own? Will my growing understanding of autism skew the results? What if I am identified as autistic? What if I am not identified as autistic? What if I am identified as something else? What if??? – the list of questions went on.

This is how my autistic journey began. An accidental intersection of television, reflection, and curiosity. These elements set into motion a series of events that would ultimately change my life for the better.

---

[10] https://www.soundmindpsych.com/

I'm Really Autistic!

In February 2020, I was evaluated for autism. I was 48 years old. Before being evaluated, I met with Dr. Brown for an initial conversation and there were questionnaires my wife and I completed before I returned to Dr. Brown's office again for the rest of the evaluation. In all, these were the tests included in my autism evaluation:
- Clinical interviews
- Wechsler Adult Intelligence Scale – Fourth Edition (WAIS-IV)[11]
- Beck Anxiety Inventory (BAI)
- Royal College of Psychiatrist Adult Autism Interview
- Behavior Rating Inventory of Executive Function[12] (BRIEF-A) – Self Report (me) and Observer Report (my wife)
- Conners Continuous Performance Test – Third Edition (CPT-3)
- Sensory Profile – Second Edition (SP-2)

I don't recall many details of the evaluation process, but I do remember it seemed to take a lot of time and that the office was a bit on the warm side. Once I finished, Dr. Brown and I had a brief conversation about next steps and I went home. A few weeks passed between the evaluation and when I returned for my results. During this time, I kept worrying about whether or not I showed my true self or if I masked too much. I also worried about if I acted too autistic, since I had studied autism quite a bit, and that Dr. Brown would find that suspicious. It was a pensive time until I returned for the final consultation.

In March, 2020, I found myself sitting across from Dr. Brown at her desk. She shared with me her final report, which was 10 pages long. She walked through each

---

[11] Intelligence measures are not necessarily part of ordinary autism evaluations; however, I was curious to learn as much about myself that we included this test to satisfy my curiosity.
[12] These were completed prior to my in-office evaluation.

page to explain her findings. I found myself stimming like hell—my knee bouncing to the point that I actually noticed. Nothing really surprised me, but I was still anxious to hear her conclusion. Her message: "Scott, I do believe you are autistic."

Though I felt really confident this would be the conclusion, it still shocked me to hear the words aloud. I recall feeling a wave of emotions from relief to anxiety to confusion and back to relief. We talked for several minutes after that, but I don't recall the substance of that part of the conversation. I do remember that Dr. Brown made me feel heard, understood, and supported. I felt no judgment or feelings of being "less." There was a calm within the core of me even as I navigated an emotional tsunami. I remember wiping tears of joy from my face as Dr. Brown talked about options moving forward. She said she felt there was no reason to seek any treatment unless I felt like I wanted to. She did provide me with some suggestions to help make sense of my autism, which included readings and a movie. I thanked her for her services and left her office.

As I walked to the parking lot to get in my truck and drive home, the emotional waves continued. They were palpable. One moment I was elated and the next I was in tears. There was confusion and clarity. I recall getting into my truck, nearly hyperventilating and crying inconsolably—not because I received "bad news," but because the moment Dr. Brown confirmed my suspicions, I felt validated! My entire life I knew I was different and now I had an answer as to why. I felt more like a whole person than I ever felt; it was both wonderful and scary at the same time. I was definitely happy with the outcome.

On the drive home I kept thinking, "How am I going to tell my wife? What is she going to think about me being autistic?" When I got home, I let her know that I was okay, but that I wanted to have some time alone, and she gladly provided that space. A short while later we went to bed and that's when I shared my experience. She was very supportive and reinforced how much she cared about me. We talked, we cried, we laughed, and we both felt a sense of comfort in the knowledge that I was formally identified as autistic.

> BEING FORMALLY IDENTIFIED AS AUTISTIC GAVE ME ANSWERS TO AND AN EXPLANATION OF MY LIFE'S EXPERIENCES.
> -DR. SCOTT FRASARD

Reproduced with permission from Brittany Gonzalez, M.Ed.

I'm Autistic; Now What?

Armed with the knowledge that someone else—and a professional at that—also believed what I had come to believe about myself, I returned to my journey of discovery with even more fervor. I revisited the resources I had encountered prior to my formal identification, looking at them again through my updated lens, but something felt incomplete or inaccurate.

At this stage of my journey, much of my focus had led me predominantly to research based on the medical or deficit model of autism[13]. My background in medicine, along with the literature I was currently delving into about autism, all seemed to underscore the notion that autism was a condition requiring treatment. It was portrayed as a negative, a deficiency. However, I didn't see myself as flawed; I was simply autistic. I didn't lack anything; I was autistic. As I continued to immerse myself in these resources, I couldn't help but feel that my own experiences and viewpoints were conspicuously absent. It was the first time I felt "othered," and it was profoundly unsettling.

Seeking a deeper understanding and a connection with voices similar to mine, I ventured beyond the predominant narratives. It was crucial for me to find perspectives that mirrored my own, not merely the insights of medical professionals, scholars, and non-autistic advocates who aimed to speak on my behalf. I turned to online communities, immersing myself in a variety of groups. Among these, I encountered environments that ranged from warmly inviting to unexpectedly contentious. The most welcoming spaces were typically those led by autistic individuals themselves, offering a sense of camaraderie and shared understanding. Conversely, the groups that felt like battlegrounds were often orchestrated by non-autistic individuals advocating on behalf of the autistic community. Each type of group played a distinct role in my ongoing journey of self-discovery and understanding.

Amidst these spaces, I began sharing my own thoughts and revelations, grappling with the newfound acknowledgement that I'm autistic. Despite knowing myself for 48 years, it was as if I were reborn and had to learn things all over again.

---

[13] The medical, or deficit, model of autism views autism as a disorder characterized by deficits or impairments in social interaction, communication, and behavior. It focuses on diagnosing and treating these deficits through medical or therapeutic interventions, aiming to reduce symptoms and help individuals conform to typical developmental standards.

The process was both empowering and daunting. Within the supportive online communities, I discovered validation and affirmation that my identity and way of being were neither flawed nor lacking. Conversely, the more contentious and divisive groups served as a catalyst for self-examination, challenging my preconceptions, and prompting introspection on what I had previously believed about autism and autistic people.

One of the most important lessons I learned was the importance of genuinely listening with an open mind to those who are actually autistic. In listening to the voices of those who were actually autistic I learned an immense amount about myself, autism, and the autistic and autism communities. I started to challenge the assumptions and preconceived notions I had brought with me about autism into this journey. As my understanding about autism grew, so did my confidence with my new understanding of myself. I found myself sharing my ah-ha moments and began to identify as an autistic self-advocate.

Not long after I started sharing my understandings and experiences as a late-identified adult in public forums, I noticed an influx of individuals reaching out to me. They sought to exchange ideas, ask me questions, and draw from my insights. This marked my transition from merely advocating for myself to becoming an actual advocate for others in the autistic community. Once I accepted that others were reflecting on my contributions, seeking my advice, and even making life decisions after considering my words, I decided that I needed to be careful with how I yielded such responsibility. It became clear to me that sharing solely from my own singular perspective would not be enough to represent a community that consists of an almost infinite range of autistic experiences. In my mind, to stick with my own perspectives would be tantamount to malfeasance. How could I—a single person with a singular set of experiences, albeit autistic experiences—be a voice for so many others whose experiences are both similar and different to mine?

A Reflective Question to Ponder

In April 2022, I embarked on a new approach to advocacy for both myself and the broader autistic community. I noticed that many autistic advocates spoke for the community by unilaterally sharing from their own perspective on what should be believed about autism. This approach often resulted in a noticeable disconnect between people with differing views. Eager to bridge this divide, I strived to move beyond being just another clamoring voice focused on proclaiming my limited view as being "fact" in a vast constellation of autistic experiences.

My goal was to ensure that the widest variety of autistic voices, as well as the voices of those with autistic loved ones, were heard and amplified. To achieve this, I committed to engaging in true dialogue with anyone in the autistic and autism communities, not just those who shared perspectives similar to my own. I recognized the importance of being open to others' differing values, beliefs, and assumptions. I had to be willing to listen to others before anyone would listen to my experiences. Thus, *A Reflective Question to Ponder* was born.

I put on my change management hat and began what was to be a year-long journey of seeking out differing perspectives. I wanted to engage with anyone and everyone who experienced autism in some form or fashion to better understand their experiences, values, beliefs, and assumptions regarding a wide range of autism-related issues. Instead of sharing my particular perspective, such as my preference for identity-first language, I asked people for *their* language preference and explored why they held those preferences. I chose not to judge, to correct, to educate from my own vantage points. I worked to foster true dialogue in a non-judgmental way in order to pave the road to trust and understanding. Through this, I enriched my own understandings of autism, the autistic community, and autistic advocacy. I became a conduit for others to both share their own perspectives and to take in others' perspectives. I was amplifying voices.

I learned a lot throughout the year. Early on, my questions focused on autism and the autistic experience. Over time, the questions I posed evolved into addressing social injustice aspects of autism. I tackled more controversial topics and challenged people to consider alternative perspectives in a Socratic-like manner. I offered hypothetical "why can't it be different?" situations to encourage thinking beyond convention. Changing people's minds wasn't the goal; the goal was to help others question for themselves those things that were largely unquestioned.

I see a momentum shift taking place in the autistic advocacy world. I see more people raising topics, including difficult topics, and challenging assumptions. I see people taking action where "that's just the way it is" once dominated. I see people willing to own their autistic identity and demand that they be treated with dignity and respect. This change is heartening, and I know my advocacy work contributes in a small, but positive, way. It is time to put more structure into my advocacy work, to further my focus on fostering meaningful dialogue and reflection. By encouraging people to question and explore, I aim to create a space where diverse perspectives are valued and where everyone can learn from one another.

The next part of this book is designed to do just that. The questions you'll encounter are meant to provoke thought, inspire reflection, and challenge your preconceptions about autism, the autistic community, and related issues. Let's embark on this journey together, embracing a new mindset that values introspection, empathy, and the shared human experience.

My Perspectives, For Context

As you read this book, you will notice that I have a particular orientation with respect to autism and the multitude of issues associated with autism. As such, allow me to take a moment to share my perspectives on a number of issues so you have context for the book's contents. In sharing these perspectives, I want to make it *explicitly* clear that while other autistics may share one or more of these perspectives with me, these perspectives are mine alone and do not necessarily represent the autistic community at large. This not a comprehensive list and are in no particular order:

- **Autistic**: I identify as autistic. Not autism, level 1. Not Aspergers. I am autistic.
- **Language**: I use identify-first language ("I am autistic"), not person-first language ("I have autism").
- **Identification**: I use the phrase "formally identified as autistic" to indicate my autistic status. I reject the term "diagnosis[14]" as this is borne from the medical model of disability.
- **Symbolism**: I use the gold infinity symbol as a representation for autism. I reject the puzzle piece symbol and the color blue to represent autism.
- **Functional labels**: I reject the use of "high-functioning" and "low-functioning" (or similar) to describe autism.
- **Model of disability**: I ascribe to the social model of disability as it relates to autism. I completely reject all tenets of the medical model of disability.
- **Communication**: I ascribe to Milton's[15] *double empathy problem* as the most accurate explanation to date for why autistic people and non-autistic people appear to have challenges communicating with one another.
- **Cause/Cure**: I ascribe to the idea that autism is a naturally occurring variation of human neurology. I vehemently reject the idea that anything "causes"

---

[14] Though I use "formally identified as autistic," you will see the term "diagnosis" (or similar) throughout this book. This is due to context and a change in my thinking over the time period when the questions were posed.

[15] Milton D. (2012). On the ontological status of autism: The 'double empathy problem'. *Disability and Society*, 27(3), 883–887. doi: 10.1080/09687599.2012.710008.

autism as though autism is an abnormality. I vehemently reject that there is, could be, or should be a "cure" for autism.

- **Competence**: I assume all people are competent, regardless of support needs or ability to communicate with spoken words.
- **Support**: I ascribe to supporting autistic people's needs when and where they require support and in ways they want that support to happen. I believe that nothing inherently needs support unless the autistic person wants support and that it is up to those around autistic people to change to support the autistic person.
- **Applied behavior analysis (ABA)**: I oppose using all behaviorism-based and operant conditioning-based "therapy" or "supports" with autistic people. I believe that nothing needs to change or be "fixed" unless the autistic person wants to change and/or be "fixed."
- **Autism awareness**: I believe we are well beyond needing to be aware of autism. Instead, we need understanding of what autism truly is, accept autism as a natural state of being, design a world that is fully inclusive of autistic people, and engage in activism to break down systems of oppression that marginalize, pathologize, and "other" autistic people. The world needs social justice for autistic people in order to be an egalitarian community.
- **Research**: I believe autism research needs to be defined and led by autistic researchers with a focus on improving the lives of autistic people rather than a focus on causes of autism and ways to reduce autistic appearances, which tend to make non-autistic people uncomfortable.
- **Authenticity**: I am proudly an autistic person and do not want or need to be "indistinguishable[16]" from non-autistic people.

---

[16] Psychologist Ole Ivar Lovaas is known for making the claim that children could be made "indistinguishable" from their typically-developing peers by putting them through years of intensive, one-on-one, behavior modification. His work gave way to applied behavior analysis.

- **Separability**: I am who I am because I am autistic. I cannot be separated from my autism and my autism cannot be separated from me.
- **Representation**: I believe that anywhere autism is the subject (directly or indirectly) or where autistic people are affected, autistic people *must* be involved in any decisions made, if not steering the dialogue. Merely "consulting with" autistic people for feedback is wholly inadequate and unacceptable.
- **Organizations**: I support autistic-established and operated organizations, such as Autistic Self Advocacy Network (ASAN), Reframing Autism, and Autism Women's Network, who work to support those things that the autistic community cares about. I fully reject organizations such as Autism Speaks and Talk About Curing Autism, who support and work towards things that go against what autistic people care about.
- **Symptoms**: I reject the notion that observable behaviors or mannerisms commonly associated with autism are "symptoms" of some sort of disease or condition. Rather, autistic people may have unique characteristics that differ from those who are not autistic. I am still a bit cautious about using the term "characteristic" even, as this may still align more closely with the medical model of disability rather than the social model of disability.

Chapter 2
Framing Autism

"Autism is as much a part of humanity as is the capacity to dream."

~ Kathleen Seidel

How we view and interact with autistic people is largely determined by how we see autism. A common way to view autism is through the medical model of disability. Through this lens, the autistic person is said to have a disorder, condition, or even a disease. This perspective turns natural behaviors of autistic people, like stimming or echolalia, into symptoms or signs of something being wrong. When we categorize autism as a disorder, the focus leans heavily towards altering or managing the way autistic people navigate their existence. The mindset is underpinned by the belief that there is a "proper" way to experience and interact with the world, suggesting that autistic individuals *must* change in order to fit better among those who are not autistic.

It doesn't have to be this way. We can, instead, choose to see autism as a variation of the human experience. Adopting this view eliminates the notion that there is a singular, proper way to experience and interact with the world. Instead, both the autistic and the non-autistic are mutually responsible for interactions. It is not solely the autistic who must modify their behavior or adapt to the environment in some way to make others around them more comfortable. This approach steers us away from describing and treating autistic people as being less than "normal" or otherwise deficient. With this, we move away from marginalizing (and even exploiting) autistics and towards a more inclusive and respectful society.

As I reflect on the years since being formally identified as autistic and all I've learned, I looked back at the Diagnostic and Statistical Manual of Mental Disorders, Fifth Edition (DSM-V) diagnostic criteria for autism. Comparing my experiences and what I've learned from others has reinforced my stance on rejecting the medical/deficit model of disability as a lens through which to view autism. I believe, as do many others, that the DSM-V criteria reflect:

- Autistics' reactions during stressful/traumatic events
- Observers' interpretations through their non-autistic lens
- Naturally occurring variations of the human experience

Stated differently, these criteria cast a negative light on a group of people simply because we are different. It creates a system where "fixes" can be employed for reasons that are not necessarily in the autistic person's best interests. It stereotypes us as incompetent unless someone helps. It often dooms us to a life that is somehow less successful, fulfilling, or important because our lives are being measured with someone else's ruler. In short, these criteria are oppressive.

Below, I've listed the DSM-V criteria for autism. I definitely do not believe they are an accurate description of autistic people, so I took the liberty of restating these in a more positive way that reflect my personal experiences as an autistic person:

INSTEAD OF: Deficits in social-emotional reciprocity
I SEE: Relates to others in their own unique way

INSTEAD OF: Deficits in nonverbal communicative behaviors used for social interaction
I SEE: Communicates in their own unique way

INSTEAD OF: Deficits in developing, maintaining, and understanding relationships
I SEE: Relates better with those who are more like them than those who are not

INSTEAD OF: Restricted, repetitive patterns of behavior, interests, or activities
I SEE: Enjoys doing certain things that bring joy

INSTEAD OF: Stereotyped or repetitive motor movements, use of objects, or speech
I SEE: Enjoys the sensations that certain activities or objects provide

INSTEAD OF: Highly restricted, fixated interests that are abnormal in intensity or focus
I SEE: Is deeply passionate about certain things

INSTEAD OF: Hyper- or hypo-reactivity to sensory input or unusual interest in sensory aspects of the environment
I SEE: Experiences sensory inputs in ways others do not

INSTEAD OF: Symptoms must be present in the early developmental period
I SEE: Learns to be themselves at any point throughout their lifetime

INSTEAD OF: Symptoms cause clinically significant impairment in social, occupational, or other important areas of current functioning
I SEE: A unique human

INSTEAD OF: These disturbances are not better explained by intellectual disability or global developmental delay

I SEE: Unique characteristics exist within everyone, which we may not fully understand

In this chapter, the questions focus on how we frame autism. The purpose of each question is to evoke deep reflection about how autism and autistic people are described, categorized, and labeled. The questions are not subdivided or organized into smaller categories, which may make reading them feel like you are jumping a bit from topic to topic. This is by design, as a strict subcategory structure may take away from the intended interrelationship exploration and critical reflection. By presenting questions in an integrated manner, my hope is to foster elements of discovery and interconnectedness that bring about deeper contemplation.

I encourage you to mark questions that you find particularly provocative or that caused you to question your values, beliefs, and assumptions. If you feel a visceral reaction to a question, this is not a bad thing! At the end of the chapter, there is a chapter wrap-up with an exercise to encourage further exploration of the questions. Take your time reading and enjoy!

Framing Autism   19

1.
Are autistic people held to a different standard as compared to non-autistic people when it comes to interacting with others (of any neurotype)?

2.
If you believe there are different standards for autistic and non-autistic people when it comes to interacting with others, which standards differ? Why?

3.
Does an autistic person's passion, compassion, humor, style, generosity, or kindness have to be what the majority of the world's population says it should be? Why or why not?

4.
If autism is classified as a "neurodevelopmental condition," then why isn't a "normally developing" brain similarly labeled as a "condition?"

5.
What differentiates autism as a "condition" when non-autistic (neuromajority) ways of being are not typically labeled as a condition?

6.
What assumptions are made when including the word "condition" to a way of being (e.g., "autism spectrum condition")?

7.
If people of all neurotypes present in an almost infinite number of ways, then why are autistic people the only ones who are referred to as being "on the spectrum?"

8.

What assumptions are made about someone when the phrase "on the spectrum" is used to reference them? From where do these assumptions originate?

9.

Is there an appropriate amount of interest-sharing when interacting with others?

10.

Is it possible for people to share too little when interacting with others? Why or why not?

11.

Does the amount of interest-sharing someone engages in provide any information about how that person's brain operates? Why or why not?

12.

How would you feel if your competence were judged based on the degree to which you engaged in interest-sharing during interactions with others?

13.

If non-autistic people experience communication difficulties, should those difficulties be used as a diagnostic criterion to differentiate them from others? Why or why not?

14.

Some people ascribe to the belief that autistic people have difficulty communicating. It's a diagnostic criterion for autism in the DSM, so it must be true, right? Implicit in this idea is that there are "correct" ways to communicate and by default, there are "incorrect" ways to communicate. Should this notion of autism be critically examined and/or challenged? Why or why not?

15.
Some individuals hold the view that autism presents across a broad continuum of severity, with some being perceived as more or less autistic than others. Should the notion that levels of autism can vary significantly among individuals be critically examined and/or challenged? Why or why not?

16.
If you believe people should NOT critically examine and/or challenge the idea that autism ranges in severity, why do you believe this to be the case?

17.
If you believe people SHOULD critically examine and/or challenge the idea that autism ranges in severity, why do you believe this to be the case?

18.
Without debating the notion of autism severity itself, what might happen if we were to critically examine and/or challenge the idea that autism ranges in severity? Who might benefit from such a debate? Who might be harmed from such a debate?

19.
What if instead of being "diagnosed with autism," people "earned an autism certification?" Would this change how autism and autistic people are perceived, especially in the workplace? Why or why not?

20.

How does changing a single word, such as replacing "diagnosed" with "certified," impact how we perceive the subject, if at all?

21.

Would a word other than "diagnosis" provide autistic people with more dignity, respect, and self-worth? Why or why not?

22.

What assumptions and stigmas are associated with the phrase "autism diagnosis?"

23.

If someone is identified as autistic via the medical model, another via the social model, and a third via self-identification, are all three rightfully autistic (all other things being equal)? Why or why not?

24.

Considering the medical model, the social model, and self-identification, is one approach to identifying autism MORE legitimate than the other two? Why or why not?

25.

Considering the medical model, the social model, and self-identification, is one approach to identifying autism LESS legitimate than the other two? Why or why not?

26.

Among the three models -- medical, social, and self-identification -- is there any one model whereby a person identified as autistic is not worthy of receiving support? If so, which one(s) and why?

27.

Are stigmas and stereotypes disabling for people to whom they are directed? Why or why not?

28.

Where do people learn stigmas and stereotypes directed towards autistic people?

29.

When an autistic person interacts with a non-autistic person through an online platform, whether synchronously or asynchronously, is the double empathy problem[17] increased, decreased, or unchanged?

30.

If a method existed to accurately and reliably identify autism (and other neurotypes) at birth, should this identity be included on one's birth certificate? Why or why not?

31.

How might including an accurate neurotype identification on one's birth certificate benefit that person?

---

[17] Milton argues that autistic and non-autistic people experience a lack of understanding for the other group, due to our vastly different experiences in the world, making for challenging communication.

32.

How might including an accurate neurotype identification on one's birth certificate harm that person?

33.

Assuming an accurate method for identifying autism at birth was possible and reliable, would you want your neurotype included on YOUR birth certificate? Why or why not?

34.

If you're autistic and could request a reissued birth certificate with "autistic" included, would you do so? Why or why not?

35.

If one's autistic identification was included on their birth certificate, should this be sufficient evidence to receive support services requiring a formal diagnosis? Why or why not?

36.

Do you feel a self-assessment instrument of autistic traits developed by autistic researchers is a positive step forward for the autistic community? Why or why not?

37.

Would your response differ if the instrument was built exclusively by non-autistic researchers? Why or why not?

38.

How could the autistic community benefit if the medical field, schools, support providers, insurance companies, and lawmakers accepted reliable self-assessment instrument results as an official autism identification?

39.

When people say, "we shouldn't let our diagnosis define us," do they mean that stereotyped characterizations of autism shouldn't be taken to heart? Why or why not?

40.

Would you want to be defined by stereotypical views of having deficiencies, potentially leading to a lifetime of being perceived as less than acceptable? Why or why not?

41.

If stereotyped deficiencies are how autistic people are represented, how do we change this perspective? Should this perspective be changed?

42.

Why is a lack of ability a dominant assumption about autistic people?

43.

Where do people learn the lack of ability assumption about autistic people?

44.

Do some cultures assume autistic people have a lack of ability more than other cultures? Why or why not?

45.

Is lack of ability a fact or false assumption about autistic people by non-autistic people?

46.

How might an autistic person feel if/when someone says, "You should not let autism define you"?

47.

How might a person respond to someone who says, "You should not let autism define you?"

48.

Would your reaction to hearing, "Autism shouldn't define you," differ based on whether the person saying this is or is not autistic?

49.

What assumptions accompany the thought that autistic people should not define themselves by their autism?

50.

Do functional labels (e.g., low and high-functioning) tell you anything about an autistic person's experiences? Why or why not?

51.

If functional labels do not provide an indication of an autistic person's experiences, why are they used so frequently?

52.
If functional labels do provide an indication of an autistic person's experiences, what precisely do they tell us?

53.
What assumptions are made about autistic people when we use functional labels?

54.
Do functional labels help non-autistic people deal with certain uncomfortable feelings about autism/autistic people? If so, what and why?

55.
Are the phrases "high-functioning autistic" (HFA) and "low-functioning autistic" (LFA) derogatory towards autistic people? Why or why not?

56.
What assumptions are made about autism and autistic people by using functional labels?

57.
Do functional labels tell us something specific or useful about an autistic person? If so, what and why?

58.
Given the ongoing debate about what autism is and is not, whether it is caused or just how the brain is, what needs to be treated or not treated, and the myriads of other considerations, is it possible to establish a holistic, accurate, and universally agreed-upon definition or description of autism? Why or why not?

59.

If there are infinitely different possible ways to be or present as autistic, can autism be succinctly described in writing? Why or why not?

60.

If we cannot succinctly describe autism as a construct, does it really exist? Why or why not?

61.

If the best we can do is to describe autistic experiences or autistic people's observable characteristics, and these differ by person, time, duration, context, etc., is there any value in trying to group these into a single category called "autism"? Why or why not?

62.

Is it wrong to think of "autism parent" as being an identity? Why or why not?

63.

What are some advantages and disadvantages of viewing "autism parent" as an identity?

64.

Does the use of the identity "autism parent" detract from "autistic" as an identity in the eyes of autistic individuals? Why or why not?

65.

Why do so many people have a strong negative reaction when they hear a psychologist or other clinician give their child an autism diagnosis?

66.

Where do parents learn to have a strong negative reaction to their child being diagnosed as autistic?

67.

What assumptions do parents have about their child at the moment their child is diagnosed as autistic? Why?

68.

What makes the moment in time when parents learn their child is autistic more negative or more positive? Why?

69.

Do you feel there is a need to categorically differentiate autistic people who have minimal an/or infrequent support needs from autistic people who have significant and/or frequent support needs? Why or why not?

70.

How does the practice of labeling autistic individuals according to their support needs impact perceptions of autism?

71.

What does it say about supporting autistic people and support services if we have to differentiate between autistic people based on support needs?

72.

Other than as required by policy or regulation constraints, is differentiation necessary in order to provide support services to autistic people? Why or why not?

73.

If the diagnostic criteria for autism were significantly narrowed such that only those with moderate to significant support needs would be identified as autistic, what would happen?

74.

Would more people benefit from a narrowed autism identification criteria? Who would benefit? Why?

75.

Would more people be harmed from a narrowed autism identification criteria? Who would be harmed? Why?

76.

How would narrowing the autism identification criteria affect those who are not autistic? Why?

77.

How would support services be impacted if the autism identification criteria were narrowed?

78.

What assumptions are made about individuals based on criteria like the DSM criteria for autism?

79.

Do you see the word "meltdown" as an infantilizing[18] descriptor for when an autistic person experiences a nervous system overload?

---

[18] To treat (someone) as a child or in a way which denies their maturity in age or experience.

80.

If you don't consider "meltdown" to be infantilizing, do you view it as derogatory in some other way when describing a nervous system overload? Why or why not?

81.

What is your reaction to the following position statement excerpt from the National Council on Severe Autism's position on diagnostic labels?

"The broadening of the construct of autism in the form of the Diagnostic and Statistical Manual (DSM-5) criteria for Autism Spectrum Disorder (ASD) in 2013, while well-intentioned, has had the effect of rendering the diagnosis essentially meaningless, as it allows for the same diagnosis to be given to wholly disparate individuals." Additionally, the organization's call to action asserts that, "…the umbrella ASD diagnosis has marginalized a growing population of individuals whose neurobehavioral pathologies are among the most alarming and disabling in the entire field of psychiatry. A revision to the DSM is clearly needed, and we urge the APA to undertake these updates as expeditiously as possible."[19]

82.

Do you agree with the National Council on Severe Autism's position on diagnostic labels? Why or why not?

83.

Does broadening the autism construct render the autistic diagnosis "essentially meaningless?" Why or why not?

---

[19] National Council on Severe Autism. (2020). *NCSA Position Statement on Diagnostic Labels: The Need for Categorical Recognition of Severe Autism in the DSM.* Retrieved from: https://www.ncsautism.org/dsm

84.

From your perspective, does a broad, overarching label of "autism" disenfranchise anyone who is autistic and also requires significant support for daily care? Why or why not?

85.

From your perspective, does a broad, overarching label of "autism" benefit someone who is autistic and does not require significant support? Why or why not?

86.

Why might the DSM criteria for autism be seen as bad, maladaptive, and/or pathological?

87.

What is your reaction to the descriptor "Excessive preoccupation with details"? Is being preoccupied with details necessarily a negative trait? Why or why not?

88.

Is "Excessive preoccupation with details" helpful in describing the autistic experience in any way? If so, how?

89.

What does the phrase "Excessive preoccupation with details," when used to characterize autistic people, reveal about the individuals who create such descriptors?

90.

In what ways can the descriptor "Excessive preoccupation with details" be harmful to autistic people?

91.

Do autistic people really possess distinct traits that are different from those who are not autistic? Why or why not?

92.

Is the phrase "autistic traits" a form of pathologizing how a person experiences the world? Why or why not?

93.

Which is a more accurate way to describe what makes autistic people different: their "traits" or their experiences of the world around them? Why?

94.

Is there a difference between "autism" as a label for a condition and "autism" as an identity for a person? Why or why not?

95.

What assumptions do you hold when regarding "autism" as a label for a condition? What has influenced those assumptions?

96.

When it comes to being autistic, which of the two statements below is more accurate?
- The way autistic people experience the world around them produces their observable behaviors.
- Autistic people's observable behaviors produce the way they experience the world around them.

97.

Why do you think some autistic people embrace autism as an identity?

98.

What assumptions do you make when viewing "autism" as an identity for a person? What helped inform those assumptions?

99.

What role does embracing one's autism/autistic identity play in advocating for the autistic community?

100.

Does being openly autistic help or harm one's own autism advocacy efforts? Why or why not?

101.

What advantages and disadvantages does embracing one's own autistic identity have on advocacy outcomes?

102.
What advantages and disadvantages does NOT embracing one's own autistic identity have on advocacy outcomes?

103.
If you're autistic, when you engage in your special interest(s), does this engagement help you manage elevated stress levels? Why or why not?

104.
If you're autistic, does engaging in your interest serve any specific purpose?

105.
If you are unable to engage with one of your interests, how does it make you feel?

106.
How do you feel when someone refers to your interest as a "special interest" versus something else without the term "special" included? Why or why not?

107.
If engaging in your interest does reduce elevated stress in your life, do you purposefully engage in your interest for the goal of stress reduction? Why or why not?

108.
For all my non-autistic colleagues, what is the worst thing that would happen if everything the medical/deficiency perspective of autism tells us is true about autism is actually false?

109.

Occasionally, there are mentions of people "faking" being autistic. Have you observed firsthand someone "faking" being autistic?

110.

Why would someone pretend to be part of a marginalized group such as autistic people? What would they gain as a result?

111.

If you have observed firsthand someone "faking" being autistic, what did the person do to fake being autistic?

112.

If you have observed firsthand someone "faking" being autistic, how did you confirm the person isn't actually autistic?

113.

Why do some people view autistics who have fewer, different, or unnoticeable support needs as being individuals who cause problems for the autistic community?

114.

Why are autistics with fewer, different, or unnoticeable support needs who advocate for themselves and others sometimes seen as problematic?

115.

Why are autistics with fewer, different, or unnoticeable support needs who are not afraid to call out ableism or abuse sometimes seen as people who cause problems?

116.
Why are autistics with fewer, different, or unnoticeable support needs who often protest ABA and call for its abolition sometimes seen as people who cause problems?

117.
Why do some view autistics with fewer, different, or unnoticeable support needs–whom they doubt are actually autistic or capable of understanding the experiences of "real" autistics–as people who cause problems?

118.
Why do some people view as problematic those autistics with fewer, different, or unnoticeable support needs who frequently raise pointed questions about systematic marginalization?

119.
Why do some people continue to view autistics who have fewer, different, or unnoticeable support needs as people who cause problems for the autistic community? More importantly, how do we stop this from continuing?

120.
If you were to be formally identified[20] (diagnosed) as autistic and all other things being equal (education, experience, qualifications, etc.), who would you rather conduct the autism evaluation and give you the news: a non-autistic psychologist or an autistic psychologist? Why?

---

[20] As noted in Chapter 1, I do not ascribe to the medical model of disability. As such, I reject language about autism that treats it as a medical condition of any sort. This is why I use "identified" instead of "diagnosed" when refereeing autism.

121.

What might differ about an autism evaluation conducted by a non-autistic psychologist as compared to an autistic psychologist?

122.

Should we abandon the pursuit of more accurately defining "autism" and describing autistic people and shift our focus on developing, implementing, and providing full access to support? Why or why not?

123.

Would autism be different if it were defined by sociologists[21] rather than psychologists? Why or why not?

124.

How would autism be conceptualized and autistic people described if this work had been done by sociologists rather than psychologists?

125.

What is the one most hurtful myth or stereotype about autism that has been directed at you or someone you know?

126.

Would the ways society at large perceive autism and autistics be better, worse, or the same if autism were defined by sociologists rather than psychologists? Why or why not?

---

[21] Sociologists are experts in and study the development, structure, and functioning of human society.

127.
Are autistic people more likely, less likely, or equally likely to be atheist as compared to non-autistic people? Why or why not?

128.
If someone is both autistic and atheist, would this mean they lack morals or have less ability to know the difference between right and wrong? Why or why not?

129.
If you believe autistic people are more likely to be atheist, why do you believe this?

130.
What would you want others to understand about the pain caused by an autism stereotype aimed at you or someone you know?

131.
How would you feel hearing about the hurt autistic people experience when a stereotype is directed towards them?

132.
If you were informed by an autistic person that something you've said or done was hurtful, how would you respond?

133.
It's a fact: some people view autism as a tragedy. But is it truly a tragedy, or is any perceived tragedy of autism specifically a self-fulfilling prophecy?

134.
Are people led to believe autism is a tragedy?

135.
If "autism as a tragedy" is a self-fulfilling prophecy, how can we erase the prophecy?

136.
Why must autistic people be ostracized to the extent that their very existence is deemed tragic?

137.
Could we erase the idea of "autism as a tragedy" by simply reframing autism?

138.
Who has the decision-making authority to decide what is "problematic" and "socially significant" behavior? Why do they have that authority?

139.
How easy or difficult is it for individuals to be formally identified (diagnosed) as autistic once they seek identification?

140.
If the process of being formally identified as autistic is difficult, what makes it difficult?
If it is easy, what makes it easy?

141.
Is it possible for someone to be absolutely 100% disability-free at any snapshot in time? Why or why not?

142.

If someone can be 100% disability-free at any snapshot in time, what would that person and context look like?

143.

If there is such thing as learning disabilities, are there also such things as:
- Teaching disabilities?
- Experiential disabilities?
- Contextual disabilities?
- Situational disabilities?
- Cooking disabilities?
- Being unique disabilities?
- And so on?

… and should these also be included in the DSM?

144.

In what ways would different definitions and understandings about what "disability" means impact whether or not someone experiences a disability?

145.

Of the following two things, which is more important for an autistic person to have and why?

- Ability to speak with words
- Confidence

146.

Are there situations where the ability to speak with words is more important than feeling confident, or vice versa? What are those situations?

147.

Why would either the ability to speak with words or the feeling of confidence be considered more important than the other in certain situations?

148.

What assumptions inform our value of speaking with words and being confident?

149.

What is the relationship between speaking with words and confidence, if any? Why does that relationship exist, if it does?

150.

When an autistic person has a deep, passionate interest in a specific topic and has studied it so thoroughly as to know more about the topic than most everyone else, it is frequently called a "special interest." When a non-autistic person has the same amount of passionate interest, it rarely, if ever, is referred to as a "special interest." Why is this, and is this a double standard?

151.

Building on question 150, could the dissertation topic of every PhD or EdD candidate be considered their "special interest"? Why or why not?

152.

What does it reveal about our assumptions of an individual when their deep passion is labeled as "special," especially within the context of an already marginalized group of people?

153.

Would using the term "special interest" to speak of a deep, passionate interest be a derogatory term if it is used exclusively with autistic people? Why or why not?

154.

If you're not autistic, how would you interpret the phrase "special interest" if someone used it to refer to a deep, passionate interest of yours? Would it feel good or bad?

155.

Are there any differences in views people hold about others who have deep passions that are cognitive[22] in nature compared to those that are psychomotor[23] in nature? Why or why not?

156.

Is autism a well-defined or poorly-defined construct? Why or why not?

157.

Are autistic people doomed to lead an unhappy, unsuccessful life if they are not identified and/or given specific therapy as a child? Why or why not?

---

[22] The cognitive domain deals with the facts, terms, concepts, ideas, relationships, patterns, conclusions, etc. of a subject.
[23] The psychomotor domain deals with the physical movement, coordination, and use of the motor-skill areas.

158.

Is the autistic community a marginalized group of people?
Why or why not?

159.

Does the perception of the autistic community being a marginalized group differ based on the group (e.g., medical professionals, caregivers, parents, autistic individuals) with which one identifies? Why or why not?

160.

What are the practical consequences if the autistic community is marginalized?
Why?

161.

If the autistic community is marginalized, what would it take for this to no longer be the case?

162.

Who are the people that assume autistic people are not capable?

163.

How do we change public perception of autistic people's capabilities?

164.

What harm does the assumption that autistic people are not capable cause the autistic community? Why?

165.
Would the late-identified adult have a better life if they were identified as autistic during childhood? Why or why not?

166.
Would the late-identified adult have a better life if they were identified as autistic during childhood *and* received therapy, in whatever form that might be? Why or why not?

167.
Would the late-identified adult have a better life if they were identified as autistic during childhood *and* received support, but not therapy? Why or why not?

168.
Why do stereotypes about autism persist?

169.
At the time a child is diagnosed as autistic, do you feel the parents receive information that instills some level of fear about the child's wellbeing or future? Why or why not?

170.
When a child is diagnosed as autistic, what information is given to parents that may instill fear? Why is this information delivered?

171.

Reflect on or imagine the emotions a parent might experience upon receiving information following their child's autism diagnosis. What do you think the nature of this information is or could be? How might it influence a parent's feelings or outlook?

172.

Do you perceive someone who rejects the medical/deficit model of disability in favor of embracing the social model as being less interested in supporting autistic people? Why or why not?

173.

The DSM was written through a particular lens—the neuromajority lens. With this in mind, one of the DSM's criteria for autism is:

"Deficits in social-emotional reciprocity, ranging, for example, from abnormal social approach and failure of normal back-and-forth conversation; to reduced sharing of interests, emotions, or affect; to failure to initiate or respond to social interactions."

If one were to interpret this criterion through the autistic's lens, would this mean that non-autistic people are autistic to autistic people? Why or why not?

174.

When it comes to supporting autistic people, how does embracing the medical/deficit model differ from embracing the social model?

175.
How does the medical/deficit model inform policy and legislation as compared to the social model?

176.
When it comes to autism, who would benefit by shifting from a medical model of disability to a social model of disability—autistic people or non-autistic people? Why?

177.
If the world shifted to a social model of disability for autism, would one group benefit at the expense of the other? Why or why not?

178.
Assuming that disability services and legal protections would still exist regardless of the model by which we view disabilities, would any harm come to anyone (especially the most vulnerable) who identifies as autistic? Why or why not?

179.
Do adults who were identified as autistic later in life tend to talk about autism more than what is "socially acceptable?"

180.
Is there a subset of the autistic population who are NOT sentient? Why or why not?

181.

What impact would the removal of Autism Spectrum Disorder by the American Psychiatric Association (APA) from the Diagnostic and Statistical Manual of Mental Disorders (DSM), the official classification of mental illnesses, have on the stigma associated with pathologizing autism?

182.

What role does the DSM play in perpetuating any real or perceived link between autism and mental illness? Why?

183.

What unintended consequences could removing autism from the DSM bring to the autistic community, if any? Why?

184.

Who would be most impacted by removing autism from the DSM? Least impacted? How could the consequences be mitigated?

185.

What positive outcomes would be realized by removing autism from the DSM? Why?

186.

Do autistic people lack social skills? If so, what specific skills? Why do you believe this?

187.
If you are an autistic adult who was identified later in life, what feelings did you experience:
- At the time you received the news?
- Over the first two days after receiving the news?
- Over the first two months after receiving the news?

188.
If you are an autistic adult who was identified later in life, did you share your identification news with anyone, and when? Why or why not?

189.
If you are an autistic adult who was identified later in life, how did others react when you shared the news of your identification? How did you respond to their reaction?

190.
If you are an autistic adult who was identified later in life, how much time passed before you became comfortable with knowing you're autistic?

191.
If you are an autistic adult who was identified later in life, would you choose to seek formal identification if you had the opportunity to do it all over again? Why or why not?

192.
What assumptions are made about "social skills" when comparing the interactions of autistic people and non-autistic people?

193.

Does it matter if people interact with others differently? Why or why not?

194.

Why might some people take exception with how autistic people interact with others?

195.

If someone takes exception to how an autistic person interacts with others, where is the source of the problem?

196.

What is your understanding of why autistic people stim[24]?

197.

What is the role or function of stimming in the lives of the autistic person?

198.

Do you believe stimming results in social isolation? Why or why not?

199.

What are your thoughts regarding this statement: "The antiquated medical paradigm thinking about autism needs to go away."

---

[24] Repetitive motions that help autistic people regulate their senses, relieve stress, relieve boredom, help with concentration, communicate something, or just plain feels good.

200.
If you were to learn for the first time today that you're autistic, which of these would be the first action you'd take? Why?

A. Get a second opinion
B. Let the news sink in
C. Seek treatment options
D. Learn more about autism

201.
Where is the dividing line between individuals who are truly autistic and individuals who are not?

202.
Do you believe autism exists on a scale of how much autism someone possesses? Why or why not?

203.
Is it necessary for support needs to be continuous (such as on a daily basis) for someone to be considered autistic, or can they be intermittent? Why or why not?

204.
Must support needs be significant for someone to be considered autistic, or can they be simple? Why or why not?

205.
If you are a medical professional, what were you taught in school regarding autistic patients?

206.

Why do social norms exist?

207.

What function do social norms serve?

208.

Is there an assumption that non-autistic people's behavior is inherently the "correct" or socially acceptable standard?

209.

What role do differences play in shaping social norms?

210.

If social norms did not exist, would societies function? Why or why not?

211.

How do social groups decide how to handle a minor deviation from social norms? What about a major deviation?

212.

How are social norms changed?

213.

How does a social group decide it's time to change a social norm?

214.

In some cultures, eye contact is socially appropriate, frequently cited as being important to clear communication and listening. At the very least, a lack of eye contact is associated with negative things, such as lying or lack of interest, but is this true of all people?

215.

If someone is completely unable to see and they did not make eye contact while speaking with someone in person, would that be socially inappropriate? Why or why not?

216.

True or false: Autism is a construct that cannot be easily defined in consistent, concrete terms.

217.

What makes someone autistic?

218.

Generally speaking, are autistic people's social skills:
- Acceptable for autistic people only?
- Acceptable for non-autistic people only?
- Acceptable for both autistic and non-autistic people?
- Not acceptable for either autistic or non-autistic people?

219.

For those who were formally identified as autistic later in life, how did that make you feel?

220.
What leads the average, everyday person to conclude that someone they've met or know is autistic? Are the conclusions drawn from visible behaviors, the way the person's brain functions, or another factor?

221.
What underlying reasons or beliefs influence a person's assumption that someone is autistic, as described in question 220?

222.
Where did we learn our reasons and beliefs about what makes someone autistic?

223.
If you are a parent of an autistic child, what prompted you to seek a formal autism evaluation for your child? If you're not a parent, what do you imagine might prompt parents to seek a formal identification for their child?

224.
What happens if an individual doesn't follow a social norm?

225.
How would you react if someone challenges a social norm's validity?

226.
How important is it to you personally that social norms are followed? Why?

227.
Have you ever questioned the purpose of a specific social norm? Why or why not?

228.
Do doctors, psychologists, or other healthcare providers paint a gloomy picture of a child's future following an autism diagnosis? If so, in what ways?

229.
For parents who choose not to seek a formal autism evaluation for their child, how does that decision affect parenting approaches, if at all?

230.
If you were taught that autism is a deficit, abnormality, or disease:

- Do you still believe this to be true? Why?
- Did you ever question what you were taught?
- Did you ever ask an autistic person what they thought?
- Do you still hear these sorts of statements? From where?
- Do you ever think that autism is just a difference?

231.
How would our world be different if society valued adjusting social norms to embrace everyone's differences?

232.
If society shifted to value and adjust social norms to embrace everyone's differences, in what ways might the world and humanity improve?

233.
If society shifted to value and adjust social norms to embrace everyone's differences, in what ways might the world and humanity deteriorate?

234.

Which of the following phrases resonates more closely with your understanding of the lived experiences of autistics?

- Abnormalities and deficits

- Environmental barriers and constraints

235.

Reflecting on question 234, what personal observations or experiences led you to the phrase that more closely resonated with you?

236.

Reflecting on question 234, what assumptions might influence someone to consider one option over the other?

237.

If you had a difficult time selecting one statement in question 234 as being true or truer than the other, what was the deciding factor in making your selection?

238.

When and where did you accept one statement in question 234 as being true or truer than the other? Has your position changed over time?

239.

In what ways must public policy and legislation change to embrace something other than a medical/deficit model of disability for autism?

240.

In what ways must autism organizations change in order to adopt and promote something other than a medical/deficit model of disability for autism?

241.
In what ways must university curricula and philosophies change in order to foster something other than a medical/deficit model of disability for autism?

242.
In what ways must support providers change in order to apply an approach other than the medical/deficit model of disability for autism?

243.
How would changing from a medical/deficit model of disability to a non-medical/deficit model of disability challenge foundational values, beliefs, and assumptions about autism and autistic people?

244.
How would you personally begin the transition from a medical/deficit model of disability to an alternative model? What would be your first step?

245.
Why are functional labels ("high-functioning", "low-functioning") not applied to non-autistic people?

246.
Is there such a thing as a low-functioning non-autistic person?

247.
Why is there no "medium-functioning" label for autistic people?

248.

What does it mean when we say someone is "high-functioning" or "low-functioning"? Does this change if we're talking about autistic people versus non-autistic people?

249.

Is there a reason it's socially acceptable to use functioning labels with autistic people (or other disabled groups, for that matter), but not for non-autistic people?

250.

Why do people use functional labels for autistic people instead of referring to more specific support needs, which could provide a more useful message about what someone may require?

251.

Would it be acceptable to refer to non-autistic people as being "high-functioning" or "low-functioning?" Why or why not?

252.

For those who embrace a deficit view of autism, why is this an appropriate way to define autistic people?

253.
What's preventing us from achieving the following reality?

- Zero stigma associated with autism or being autistic
- Full acceptance of autistic individuals just as they are by non-autistic people
- Ample support and adjustments for the needs of autistic people being readily available and implemented

254.
What is one action you can take today to help make the goals in question 252 a reality?

255.
How does a deficit view of autistic people benefit them? How does it benefit non-autistic people? How does it benefit humanity at large?

256.
What harm can come to autistic people by viewing autism through the medical model of disability?

257.
What implicit and explicit assumptions are there when one views autism through the medical model?

258.
If someone self-identifies as being autistic, but doesn't fit the picture defined by the medical/deficit model, are they actually autistic? Why or why not?

259.

What are the advantages and disadvantages, if any, of using a medical model of autism over a social model of autism for autistic people?

260.

If you could change anything about the medical model of autism, what would it be? Why?

261.

What assumptions do you have about viewing autism through the social model of disability?

262.

Should the medical model of disability be the only formally acceptable approach to identifying autism?

263.

What differences exist between specific behaviors exhibited by autistic people and the exact same behaviors of non-autistic people, if any?

264.

When you hear about the "risk of autism," what does this mean to you?

265.

If you use "risk" in the context of autism, how did you come to learn this? From where did you learn this?

266.

What is really meant when people say someone is at risk of developing autism?

267.

Why do some people use the term "risk" when speaking about autism?

268.

Who gets to define appropriate social skills?

269.

Must social skills achieve unanimous approval to be considered valid, or is a lesser degree of consensus acceptable? If so, what level of agreement is sufficient?

270.

Are social skills among autistic people considered fully acceptable within the autistic community, without the need to change to align with majority norms?

271.

To achieve success, is it necessary for a person to socialize with others in a way that adheres to an arbitrarily defined, majority-set way?

272.

How much variance in social skills is acceptable?

273.

Do social skills evolve and change over time?

274.

Is it permissible for subpopulations of people to have different social skill expectations? Why?

275.
Are some social skills non-negotiable while others have an acceptable variance of expression?

276.
Is it possible for someone to display a social skill in a unique way that is still considered acceptable by others who express it more conventionally? Why or why not?

277.
When some social behaviors are common among a small minority of the population, but not the majority of the population, can they be considered appropriate for that minority population?

278.
Is it ever appropriate to engineer someone's social skills to fit in with the majority, despite it not fitting the individual's perspective of what's appropriate? Why or why not?

279.
Should an individual be discouraged or prevented from naturally expressing a social skill, like stimming for emotional regulation, if it does not harm others?

280.
With which of these two autism-related theories are you familiar?
- Double empathy problem (DEP)
- Theory of mind[25] (ToM)

281.
Between the double empathy problem and the Theory of Mind, which do you believe best explains the interactions between autistic and non-autistic people? Why?

282.
How did you come to learn about the double empathy problem and the Theory of Mind, if you are familiar with these concepts?

283.
Are there aspects of the double empathy problem or the Theory of Mind that are potentially damaging to autistic people? What, how, and why?

284.
Are there aspects of the double empathy problem or the Theory of Mind that are potentially beneficial to autistic people? What, how, and why?

285.
Should the term "disorder" be removed from formal autism diagnoses? Why or why not?

---

[25] Theory of Mind is the cognitive capacity to think about mental states, including emotions, beliefs, desires and knowledge, both our own and of others. It is not only *thinking about thinking*, but also predicting or explaining behavior based on our guesses.

286.

For those who use functional labels (high-functioning or low-functioning) when referring to an autistic person:

- What is the message you intend to convey?
- How does this descriptor add value to the conversation?
- How does the person you refer to as high- or low-functioning feel about that label? Have you asked them?

287.

In what ways have people misinterpreted your meaning of the terms high- or low-functioning?

288.

When using the terms high- and low-functioning, how do you know that the recipient of your intended message understands what you mean?

289.

What problems could arise if the term high- or low-functioning are misinterpreted by others?

290.

How did you come to learn the terms high-functioning and low-functioning?

291.

What alternative phrase or phrases could you use instead of "high-functioning" or "low-functioning" to convey your message in a more precise way to eliminate any misinterpretations or stereotypes?

292.

Is there anything wrong with saying "They need help brushing their hair and teeth" or "They cannot communicate with spoken words" instead of "They are low-functioning" when referring to an autistic person? Why or why not?

293.

Why would someone say "You are more than your diagnosis" or "You are not your diagnosis" to a person who refers to themselves as autistic?

294.

When speaking about an autistic person to someone who has no concept of autism, how would you explain the phrase "on the spectrum" so they understand what you mean?

295.

Should people previously diagnosed with "Asperger's Syndrome"[26] continue to use the term "Asperger's", or should they use "Autistic" instead?

296.

Should we stop using the term "Aspergers" despite "Asperger's Syndrome" being the official diagnosis at the time of diagnosis?

297.

Is someone with less support needs "less autistic" than someone with more support needs?

---

[26] "Aspergers" was officially removed from the Diagnostic and Statistical Manual of Mental Disorders (DSM) with the publication of the DSM-V in 2013. It was removed from the International Classification of Diseases (ICD) with the publication of the ICD-11 in 2022.

298.

If you are or identify as autistic, what sort of things have you experienced that you felt pathologized or infantilized you as a neurodivergent? How did the experience impact you?

299.

Some organizations use emotional intelligence as a measure to identify leaders and leader success. Does this practice unfairly disadvantage autistic and/or other neurodivergent people?

300.

What are some examples of social "norms" or customs in the workplace that autistic people could find confusing? What would reduce or eliminate the confusion?

301.

What socially significant behaviors (behaviors that can improve the life experience of an individual) would be common in a primarily autistic group that would not be common in a primarily non-autistic group?

Chapter 2 Wrap-Up

Having explored the questions in this chapter, take a moment to reflect on the insights and perspectives you've encountered. Revisit the chapter to note the specific question numbers that resonate with your thoughts or experience:

1. Which five questions surprised you the most?

2. Which five questions made you feel angry?

3. Which five questions made you feel sad?

4. Which five questions made you feel happy?

5. How did this chapter make you rethink the ways in which society frames autism?

6. How might you reframe autism yourself?

Chapter 3

Talking About Autism

"You have to be the bravest person in the world to go out every day, being yourself when no one likes who you are."

~ Matthew Dicks

For 22 years, I was in the medical field as a paramedic, both in the clinical setting and as an educator. In that field, practitioners must be able to deal with every conceivable illness and injury the human body can experience. We must be psychologically and emotionally capable of handling the trauma we are exposed to, for the benefit of our patients as well as our own health. We must learn to set aside our natural inclination to recoil in fear or disgust when faced with grotesque situations while remaining empathetic. Yet, in all those years and countless medical encounters, one thing stands out as being uncomfortable: talking about autism.

Throughout my medical career, I was taught that autism was a disease and/or disorder that affected people in profound ways. I came to believe that autistic people were like the stereotypical "Rain Man"[27] character, completely dependent upon others and with no hope for a "normal" life. I was led to believe that autism was a tragedy that left parents and families in ruin. Autism and autistic people were subjects that people did not like talking about, and when such topics did arise, they quickly ran their course. In these conversations, euphemisms were commonplace, such as "on the spectrum," to avoid using the word "autistic," thus avoiding

---

[27] A fictional autistic savant character in the 1988 movie, played by actor Dustin Hoffman.

negative feelings in those who were speaking of autistic people. I accepted, without question, the medical model perspective of autism, which would later contribute to some of my roller-coaster emotional experiences as I learned about being autistic myself.

Fortunately, I'm someone who is open to new perspectives and am prepared to evolve my own worldviews in light of them. There were several years that separated my departure from the medical field and learning I was autistic. This provided me with necessary space to reduce my previously held values, beliefs, and assumptions about autism and to explore autism through a different lens. Most importantly, it enabled me to listen to other autistic people and learn about the challenges they face in a world that offers little comfort to them. In time, learning from other autistic people allowed me the strength to actually talk about autism in ways that did not pathologize or marginalize autistic people.

I cannot overstate how important it is to be able to have frank conversations about autism. Having conversations about autistic people's experiences and listening to them is critical to helping them lead happier, more fulfilling lives. It's also crucial for these conversations to be true dialogues, where individuals set aside their own views to genuinely listen to others' perspectives, instead of discussions where both sides attempt to convince the other why their perspective is correct. When non-autistics assert their perspectives while autistic perspectives are silenced or marginalized, it results in the invalidation of the lived experiences of autistic people. Being regularly silenced or marginalized by the cacophony of outside voices is exhausting. No one can fully understand what the autistic experience is like unless they are autistic. I learned this for myself and realized that the vast majority of what I thought I knew about autism was actually incorrect.

It took time for me to feel comfortable talking about autism. There are many stigmas and stereotypes that need to be dismantled before autistics can truly be equals in society; however, the only way this can happen is by talking about autism, autistic people, and the autistic experience. These conversations, and the larger autistic narrative, must absolutely include and be driven by autistic people. Autistic and non-autistic people alike must seek to understand others' perspectives in order to share their own. Everyone must set aside their own perspectives to freely explore others' views, understand why people hold them, and search for the "truth," not just non-autistic people. It's a tough thing to do, given that autistic people have been subject to immense subjugation, trauma, and systematic marginalization, making it difficult for us to not include these experiences in the conversation.

In this chapter, questions focus on how we talk about autism and autistic people in our respective societies. Like the previous chapter, the purpose of each question is to evoke deep reflection about how autism and autistic people are described, categorized, and labeled. The questions are not subdivided into smaller categories, which may make reading them feel like you are jumping from topic to topic. At the end, there is a chapter wrap-up with an exercise to encourage further exploration of the questions. Take your time reading and enjoy!

302.

If Theory of Mind is correct, why is it correct?

303.

Does a lack of Theory of Mind stem from autistics, who lack the ability to attribute subjective mental states to themselves and to others, or does it stem from non-autistics, who are vague, are not direct, are polite instead of truthful, or don't always say what they mean?

304.

Generally speaking, do people dislike using the words "autistic" and "autism" because it makes them feel uncomfortable?

305.

If the words "autistic" and "autism" are uncomfortable words, why do these words make people feel uncomfortable?

306

If the words "autism" and "autistic" make people feel uncomfortable, where do we start to help people feel comfortable using the words?

307.

Should autistic people and caregivers for autistic people be curious about what supporters of behaviorism-based treatments think regarding autism and why they believe these treatments are appropriate? Why or why not?

308.
Why is it beneficial to explore and question the thoughts and beliefs of those who support behaviorism-based therapies for autistic people? What advantages come from understanding their reasons for backing these methods?

309.
Why might it be disadvantageous for people to explore and question the views of those who support behaviorism-based therapies for autistic individuals? What potential drawbacks could arise from understanding their reasons for backing these methods?

310.
Does being curious about the thoughts and beliefs of behaviorism-based therapy supporters imply that autistic people are not being true to their own identity? Does it mean that they support such treatment themselves?

311.
Can autistic people mount a meaningful argument against behaviorism-based treatments for autism without understanding why supporters of these methods support them? Why or why not?

312.
What is a quote from an autistic advocate that resonates deeply with you? Why does it hold special significance to you?

313.
If you're autistic, how do your interactions with others online compare to those in person? Why do you think that is?

314.

If you are NOT autistic, how do your interactions with others online compare to those in person? Why do you think that is?

315.

How is empathy expressed differently online compared to in person, if at all? Why do you think this is the case?

316.

Do you feel comfortable being your full authentic self on social media platforms? Why or why not?

317.

Why might autistic people feel uncomfortable being their full authentic selves on social media platforms? What possible consequences prevent them from doing so?

318.

Are social media platforms somewhere an autistic person should not be their authentic autistic self? Why or why not?

319.

What benefits are there for being one's authentic autistic self on social media platforms?

320.

How can autistic people help non-autistic people understand autism and autistic people?

321.

Does contemporary applied behavior analysis use Pavlov's work to inform their research? What evidence or reasoning do you have to support your answer?

322.

Do you think people can trust findings from a quasi-experimental study on multiple treatments that involves between two and six participants, lacks a control group, and uses either no quantitative methods or inappropriate ones to assess the treatments' effectiveness and causality? Why or why not?

323.

For those who use, prefer, and/or endorse person-first language (PFL), if using identity-first language (IFL) meant stigmas about autism and autistic people would be significantly reduced or completely eliminated, would you fully adopt IFL? Why or why not?

324.

If you learned that PFL contributed to and perpetuated stigmas, would you continue to use PFL? Why or why not?

325.

What research have you come across that supports or refutes the use of either PFL or IFL? What were the findings of that research?

326.

For those diagnosed with Asperger's, did you start identifying as autistic after the DSM removed the Asperger's diagnosis and integrated it with autism spectrum disorder?

327.
If you did change from using "Asperger's" to using "autistic," why did you do so?

328.
If you have not changed from using "Asperger's" to using "autistic," why not?

329.
If you still use the term Asperger's, do you view it as an identity? Why or why not?

330.
If you still use the term Asperger's, do you view it as being distinctly different from autism? Why or why not? What is different?

331.
If you continue to use the term "Asperger's," do you prefer person-first language or identity-first language?

332.
When referring to autism, how do you understand the word, "spectrum?"
- There are a wide variety of ways autism presents
- There is a range of autism severity

333.
What leads you to understand the word "spectrum" in the context of autism in the way that you do? Is it based on personal experiences, educational background, or some other source of information?

334.
What assumptions do you make about the word "spectrum" when it comes to referring to autism? Where did you form those assumptions?

335.
Does the word "spectrum," as it relates to autism, ever give negative perceptions or feelings? Why or why not?

336.
If you don't use the word "spectrum" when referring to autism, why not?

337.
To what extent do you agree with the statement: "To make progress to advance autistic people's human rights starts with the words we use."

338.
If you could give autism a different name, something that is more aligned to the autistic's lived experiences, what new word would you use or create? Why that word?

339.
Would anything change about how autistic people were perceived if "condition" was not included in any descriptive language regarding autism? Why or why not?

340.
If your new word for autism was a more textbook, publication-ready, or otherwise scholarly word, what fun, whimsical, or just plain catchy word would you create?

341.
If your new word for autism was more of a fun, whimsical, or just plain catchy word, what would be a more textbook, publication-ready, or otherwise scholarly word would you create?

342.

What does it mean to you when you see the phrase "Nothing about us without us?"

343.

Does adopting a "Nothing about us without us" mindset limit the autistic community? Why or why not?

344.

Does adopting a "Nothing about us without us" mindset empower the autistic community? Why or why not?

345.

What things have you experienced that truly embody the "Nothing about us without us" mindset?

346.

What assumptions do you have about those who use the #NothingAboutUsWithoutUs hashtag?

347.

How does the autistic community balance individual preferences for language with the collective goal of changing societal perceptions and interactions with autistic people?

348.

If "person with autism" is acceptable language, is "person without autism" also acceptable language? Why or why not?

349.
If you're not autistic and someone referred to you as a person without autism, how would you react? Why?

350.
How could the dynamics of power and influence change if non-autistic people were commonly described as "without autism"? What implications would this have?

351.
Over time, could describing individuals as "without autism" lead to stigmatization within this group? Why or why not?

352.
When was the last time you engaged an autistic person, asking questions to better understand their lived experiences? What did you learn?

353.
If you have engaged an autistic person to learn about their lived experiences, how did asking questions impact you? How did the answers impact you?

354.
If you have asked an autistic person about their experiences, did you change anything about how you interact with autistic people?

355.
If you have not asked an autistic person about their experiences, what's stopping you from asking?

356.
Do you have any concerns about learning something that is incongruous with your understanding of autism? If so, what are your concerns? Why?

357.
If you had an opportunity to ask an autistic person something about their experiences, what would you ask?

358.
Is it considered bad to have a positive perspective about autism or autistic people? Why or why not?

359.
How do assumptions about autism differ if one has a positive perspective about autism as opposed to a negative perspective?

360.
What are the benefits of having a positive perspective about autism or autistic people? Why?

361.
What are the consequences of having a negative perspective about autism or autistic people? Why?

362.
Does having a positive perspective about autism or autistic people equate to "romanticizing autism"?

363.
Within the autistic community, how important is it to have consistent language about autism, autistic people, being autistic, and the autistic experience?

364.
Which term most accurately describes when an autistic person is overwhelmed to the point of "acting out"?
- Nervous system overload
- Exhibiting distress behaviors
- Meltdown
- Something else

365.
What assumptions are there about the word "meltdown" to describe "challenging" behaviors?

366.
How would you like to see discussions around the language used to describe autism evolve? Why?

367.
Which specific discussions about the language used regarding autism are beneficial? Why?

368.
Which specific discussions about the language used regarding autism are NOT beneficial? Why?

369.

What assumptions do people hold about autism-associated language?

370.

Is evolving autism-associated language a good thing or bad thing for the autistic community? Why?

371.

If everyone woke up tomorrow and nobody on earth had ever heard of neurodivergences such as autism, ADHD, dyslexia, Tourette's, etc., would:
- Society conceptualize different neurotypes?
- The word "autism" even exist?
- Society view the psychology and psychiatric fields differently?
- Humanity be different?
- The DSM and ICD differ?
- People be happier or sadder?

372.

Would you want to live in a world as described in question 371? Why or why not?

373.

If you were suddenly a different neurotype (a non-autistic who is suddenly an autistic or an autistic who is suddenly non-autistic), would you be the same person? Why or why not?

374.

How does our neurotype influence who we are fundamentally?

375.
Does being open-minded and curious about others' perspectives on an issue mean you are not committed to your position on that issue? Why or why not?

376.
Are there certain topics that one should never consider open for discussion or exploration of others' perspectives? Why or why not?

377.
Does listening to and exploring perspectives that significantly differ from your own put you at risk of changing your stance on any given matter? Is such a change a good thing or a bad thing?

378.
Does listening to and exploring others' perspectives expose a person to being taken advantage of? Why or why not?

379.
How do you feel when someone you know, who shares your perspectives on a highly sensitive issue, actively seeks to understand the opposite perspective through dialogue? Why?

380.
How does listening to and exploring others' perspectives on any given issue help you refine your own worldview? Is this a good or bad thing?

381.
Why do some people feel being asked questions to understand a request or statement is anything other than simply seeking to understand?

382.

When you are asked questions to understand a statement you made, do you provide a direct answer to the specific question asked or do you include additional context to try and explain your statement in a different way? Why or why not?

383.

What assumptions do people make about those who ask clarifying questions? Why do people hold those assumptions?

384.

Do you feel being asked questions to understand your request or statement is anything other than simply seeking to understand? Why or why not?

385.

At birth, it's generally assumed that we are neurologically similar to others (neurotypical), and we are considered as such until an evaluation might determine otherwise (neurodivergent). However, what would happen if the assumption at birth was that we are neurodivergent, and only through future evaluation could we be deemed neurotypical?

386.

How would assuming each person is neurodivergent at birth, requiring an evaluation to be deemed neurotypical, change how we view neurodiversity? Why?

387.

How would assuming each person is neurodivergent at birth, requiring an evaluation to be deemed neurotypical, change how we view neurodivergent people? How would it change how we view neurotypical people?

388.
How, if at all, would assuming every child is neurodivergent at birth, requiring an evaluation to be deemed neurotypical, change the way parents and other caregivers raise children? Why?

389.
How would the assumption that each person is neurodivergent at birth, thereby requiring an evaluation to be deemed neurotypical, influence the healthcare system? Why?

390.
How would the assumption that each person is neurodivergent at birth, thereby requiring an evaluation to be deemed neurotypical, influence policies related to support services, insurance coverage, and so forth? Why?

391.
If we start with the assumption that everyone is neurodivergent at birth and only consider someone neurotypical after an evaluation, how might this shift our approach to behavioral "treatments?" Would they be aimed at helping neurotypical children adapt to neurodivergent social norms? Why or why not?

392.
Why does society prioritize individual development and advancement when our existence is deeply rooted in connections and relationships?

393.
What benefits could we experience by shifting our focus towards nurturing diverse relationships and community connections, rather than solely emphasizing personal achievement?

394.
How would our view of human life change if we all took equal responsibility for our actions together, instead of focusing on individual blame or comparison?

395.
If you're autistic, how would you want someone to respond to you if you were to tell them you're autistic? Why?

396.
What is the best response you've ever received when you shared that you or someone you love is autistic?

397.
What's the most surprising yet positive response you've received upon sharing that you or a loved one are autistic?

398.
Why might it be important to you to get certain responses from people when you share that you or someone you love are autistic?

399.
What is it about autism as an identity that has polarized the narratives among autistic people, non-autistic people, and the autistic community as a whole?

400.
Is the autistic community's interests being helped or hindered by the current autistic narratives?

401.

Do you perceive referring to someone as "autistic" as a negative, positive, or neutral thing? Why?

402.

What's stopping us from supporting autistic people in ways that help rather than harm them?

403.

The autistic community has made their perspectives known about applied behavior analysis and continue to do so, supporting these perspectives with evidence. Will the world accept these perspectives from those who are actually autistic, and if so, when? If not, why not?

404.

Which of these two books would you rather read to learn about autism?

Book A: Written by a scholar that goes into detail of every biological facet of autism as viewed through a medical lens, to include causes and treatments

Book B: Written by an autistic author that goes into detail about every facet of their lived experiences, other autistics' lived experiences, and how to best support autistics

Why did you select that book?

405.

Refer to the image below. What differences do you notice between the two search results depicted?[28]

can an autistic person	can a neurotypical person
can an autistic person - Bing Search	can a neurotypical person - Bing Search
can an autistic person **drive**	**what is** a neurotypical person
can an autistic person **become a doctor**	**define** neurotypical person
can an autistic person **get married**	neurotypical person **meaning**
can an autistic person **be a lawyer**	neurotypical person**ality disorder**
can an autistic person **be an empath**	neurotypical person **definition**
can an autistic person **own a gun**	
can an autistic person **fall in love**	
can an autistic person **join the military**	

406.

What's stopping us from creating a world where autistic people are not marginalized, but accepted for who they are?

407.

What's stopping us from changing societal norms to be inclusive of autistic people, rather than favoring some notion of "normal?"

408.

How young is too young to tell a child they are autistic? Why?

---

[28] These lists were the result of an online search I conducted for this question using the search phrases "can an autistic person" and "can a neurotypical person" to see how the search engine would complete the phrase.

409.
What are the most important considerations to take into account when telling a child they are autistic? Why are these important?

410.
If you would not tell a child they are autistic, why not?

411.
If someone holds a perspective with which you passionately disagree, would you listen to them to understand it, or would you not listen to their perspective at all? Why?

412.
Does listening to another's perspective mean you must change your perspective? Why or why not?

413.
Does the subject matter of an opposing perspective influence your willingness to listen to another's perspective? If yes, what factors contribute to this decision? Why?

414.
If another person's perspective differs from yours, does that mean their perspective is not valid? Why or why not?

415.
What would make you want to ask about someone else's perspectives when they don't match yours?

416.

What would stop you from wanting to ask about someone else's perspectives when they don't match yours?

417.

Is it possible to have a productive conversation about a specific topic with someone whose perspectives differ from yours? Why or why not?

418.

Can someone's perspective be true for them but not true for others? Why or why not?

419.

Do the statements, "All perspectives are valid" and "All perspectives are correct" mean the same thing? Why or why not?

420.

Are there some contexts in which the statements "All perspectives are valid" and "All perspectives are correct" mean the same thing while in other contexts they do not? Why or why not?

421.

What makes differing perspectives difficult to accept at times?

422.

What can we learn from differing perspectives, if any?

423.

Who gets to decide what is true and what is not true? Why?

424.

When someone asserts something is the absolute truth that you do not believe is true at all, which of the two responses below would produce a better outcome for both you and them?

A. Assert your position more adamantly than they asserted theirs to prove you're right.

B. Engage in a cordial dialogue with them to learn why they believe their position is the truth.

425.

Which of these two statements do you believe would result in greater understanding, acceptance, and changed opinions about identity-first language (IFL) and person-first language (PFL)?

Statement A: A majority of autistic people prefer IFL; you shouldn't use PFL.

Statement B: Why do you prefer PFL? Have you asked an autistic person which language they prefer and why?

426.

How do you think a person would react to each of the approaches described in question 425? Why?

427.

What emotions would each approach described in question 425 elicit? Why?

428.

If you had a strong preference for PFL or IFL, and someone tried to convince you the other was the only appropriate language, how would you respond? Why?

429.

When you encounter materials like lists or graphics highlighting desirable traits of "effective people," how do they make you feel? What about them prompts your reaction?

430.

We often hear the autistic community being described as a vulnerable population, but have you ever stopped to consider why?

431.

Why are autistic people considered a vulnerable population?

432.

To what or whom are autistic people vulnerable?

433.

If autistic people are vulnerable, is it primarily due to specific characteristics, differences, or inabilities widely perceived to be associated with autism? Why or why not?

434.

If autistic people are vulnerable, is it due more to environment, context, and non-autistic people rather than intrinsic factors? Why or why not?

435.

Is a non-autistic person's deep, passionate interest the same thing as what is often referred to as an autistic person's "special interest?" Why or why not?

436.

If the things described in question 435 are different, what makes them different?

437.

If the things described in question 435 are the same, what makes them the same?

438.

If someone is thought to have a deep passionate interest but then is formally identified as autistic, would that deep, passionate interest become a "special interest?" Why or why not?

439.

Without knowing anything about someone, would you assume they were autistic if you were told they have a "special interest?" Why or why not?

440.

How important is it to understand others' perspectives about an issue as part of helping them see a different perspective about that issue?

441.

If you have strongly held beliefs about something, how do you feel when someone tells you your beliefs are incorrect?

442.

Whose perspectives would you be more inclined to explore:
- Someone who is genuinely curious about your perspectives
- Or -
- Someone who is only interested in telling you their perspectives?

443.

When someone asks a thoughtful question about something about which you are passionate, how does that make you feel? Why?

444.

Can you trust someone who has a different perspective from yours if they are not interested in exploring your perspective? Why or why not?

445.

Does asking about perspectives that differ from yours mean that you are not being true to your own perspectives? Why or why not?

446.

What do the terms "neurotypical" and "neurodivergent" mean to you?

447.

Do the terms "neurotypical" and "neurodivergent" reflect actual differences in brain functions, or do they primarily serve to uphold and reinforce societal and medical norms? Why do you think this is the case?

448.
As an autistic, if you could go back in time and could give your younger self a single piece of advice about being an autistic adult, what would you tell your younger self? Why?

449.
If a movie or television show character is autistic, should the role be played by an autistic actor or is it acceptable for any actor to play the role? Why?

450.
What are the advantages and disadvantages of an autistic actor versus a non-autistic actor playing the role of an autistic character?

451.
What assumptions do people hold about autistic people being actors? Why do they have these assumptions?

452.
What would casting a non-autistic actor to play an autistic character say about autistic people in the larger autistic narrative? Why?

453.
Are there any topics about autism that are too taboo to talk about in any sort of conversation? Why or why not?

454.
If there are topics about autism that should never be discussed, what are they? Why should they not be discussed?

455.

What is the most uncomfortable thing to talk about when it comes to autism, and why?

456.

What would make it easier to talk about autism? Why?

457.

What is not talked about regarding autism, but should be? Why?

458.

When you hear the word "hope" in the autism/autistic context, what is the first thing that comes to your mind? Why?

459.

What assumptions do you have about the word "hope" in the autism/autistic context?

460.

Generally speaking, when people hear that someone is autistic, is there an automatic assumption that the autistic person is incapable of performing certain tasks or achieving lofty goals?

461.

If there is an automatic and widespread assumption that autistic people are generally incapable of performing certain tasks or achieving lofty goals, why is this so?

462.
If you do not believe there is an automatic and widespread assumption that autistic people are generally incapable of performing certain tasks or achieving lofty goals, why not?

436
What underlying assumptions underpin the belief that autistic people are generally incapable of performing certain tasks or achieving lofty goals?

464.
Do you think learning about autistic people accomplishing tasks or achieving goals stereotypically thought to be beyond their capabilities would alter society's perception about autistic people? Why or why not?

465.
Why do autistic people and non-autistic people tend to focus on significantly different topics and narratives regarding autism?

466.
Why do so many people feel the need to speak in euphemisms (e.g., "she is on the spectrum") rather than speaking directly ("she's autistic")?

467.
Have you ever felt uncomfortable talking about autism? If so, what made you feel that way?

468.

Which conversation is easier to have with a child aged 2 to 4?
- People dying
- Being autistic

Why did you select your answer?

469.

At what age does it begin to be easier to talk to a child about death?

470.

At what age does it begin to be easier to talk to a child about being autistic?

471.

Is it easier to talk to a child about them being autistic or about another child being autistic? Why?

472.

If you were to be formally identified as autistic as a child, say around age three, would you want your parents to tell you? Why or why not?

473.

If you were to be formally identified as autistic later in childhood, say around age 10, would you want your parents to tell you? Why or why not?

474.

As a parent, what factors would you consider in deciding whether to tell your child about their being autistic? Why are these things important to you?

475.
As a parent, what factors would make you decide to NOT tell your child they are autistic? Why would these factors lead you to feel this way?

476.
Have you ever been part of or overheard a conversation about autism and were unable to engage due to feeling uncomfortable? If so, what was the reason for this feeling?

477.
When you talk to others about autism, does who you're speaking with change what you say? Why or why not?

478.
During conversations about autism, which topics come to mind that you'd like to share but ultimately refrain from doing so? Why don't you share them?

479.
What would help you feel more comfortable talking about autism?

480.
Is there ever a time when people should NOT engage in a dialogue about autism? Why or why not?

481.
How does it feel to engage with someone about autism when they share perspectives that differ from yours?

482.
Are you uncomfortable engaging in a conversation about autism? Why or why not?

483.
Would you join others in exploring multiple perspectives about autism? Why or why not?

484.
Could the continued use of the term "spectrum" to describe autistic people be causing harm to them in ways that economically benefit others? Why or why not?

485.
How do you feel about the term "spectrum," when used to describe autistic people, possibly resulting in their harm for the economic benefit of others?

486.
Assuming a sentient computer is possible, what ethical considerations are associated with addressing its concerns about its own life? Why?

487.
How, if at all, are the ethical considerations in question 486 similar to ethical considerations of autistic peoples' lives (especially those with high support needs)?

488.
What lessons can we learn about ethical interactions with sentient computers that we can apply to ethical interactions with autistic people?

489.
How accurate is this statement: "People who have experienced a high degree of exclusion are experts in recognizing exclusionary practices." Why?

490.
Does being excluded in a particular context (like being autistic) enable one to more readily identify exclusion in other contexts (e.g., gender, race, sexual orientation, access to services)? Why or why not?

491.
How does recognizing exclusion benefit those who are excluded? How does recognizing exclusion benefit those who might exclude others, whether intentionally or unintentionally?

492.
Takiwātanga is the Māori word for autism and translates to "In their own time and space." Is this a positive or negative view of autism? Why?

493.
If you're autistic, what does "In their own time and space" mean to you?

494.
If you're not autistic, what does "In their own time and space" mean to you?

495.
How does the Māori conceptualization of autism align or differ with the medical/deficiency model of autism?

496.
Could the autistic community be part of the barrier preventing productive dialogues about autistic people's needs for change?

497.
Generally speaking, are people capable of seeing perspectives other than their own, regardless of the topic at hand? Why or why not?

498.
How important is it to see differing perspectives when trying to solve complex problems?

499.
If one has a strongly held position on a topic without any intention of changing their position, what benefit is there to understanding differing opinions?

500.
What vulnerabilities might one experience by listening to others' perspectives on any given topic?

501.
When reading a book, article, or research about autistic experiences, how important is it to you that the author or authors are actually autistic? Why?

502.
Which is the most effective way to get others—especially those with strongly held beliefs that differ from yours—to listen to your perspectives?

503.

What assumptions do you have about neurotypical language, non-autistic language, and socially acceptable behaviors? Why?

504.

If someone said that a puzzle-piece symbol and related imagery for autism is associated with negative implicit bias and connotations, would you believe them? Why or why not?

505.

Do you prefer person-first language (PFL) or identity-first language (IFL) when speaking about autism? Why?

506.

If you're a parent, does your language preference differ when speaking about your autistic child? What does your child prefer?

507.

What, if anything, would you change about the current autism narrative?

508.

What is the relationship between the type of language used, either person-first (PFL) or identity-first (IFL), and the presumed competence of autistic people?

509.

Society often suggests that being labeled as "autistic" can limit a person's life experiences and prevent them from reaching their full potential. This rationale is frequently cited as a reason for using person-first language or to force autistic people to be conditioned to appear as their non-autistic peers.

Doesn't this imply, then, that society is purposefully reducing and limiting opportunities for success available to autistic people simply because they're autistic? Why or why not?

510.

Does the use of IFL or PFL influence the non-autistic person's perceptions of autistic people's competence? Why or why not?

511.

Does the way we talk about autistic people ("Scott is autistic" versus "Scott has autism") unconsciously skew our perception of ability? Why or why not?

512.

Have you ever assessed your own perceptions of autistic people when using one language or the other? What was the result?

513.

If you are a proponent of person-first language (PFL) and when speaking to an autistic person, they politely ask you to use identity-first language (IFL), at least with them, how would you respond?

515.
When someone shares with you that they are autistic, is it better to believe them or to ask for proof? Would this differ in work versus non-work contexts? Why or why not?

516.
Would you outright reject someone's claim of being autistic in any circumstance? Why or why not?

517.
If you did not believe someone's claim of being autistic and you ask for proof, how would you react if they could support their claim with evidence?

518.
Would you accept someone's claim of being autistic if they provided evidence, or would you scrutinize their evidence? Why or why not?

519.
What would you need to believe someone's claim to being autistic? Why would these be persuasive to you?

520.
Do you believe one of the following best explains what someone might observe of an autistic person? If so, which one and why?
- Theory of Mind (ToM)
- Double empathy problem

521.

Is one theory (ToM or double empathy problem) more representative of the autistic experience than the other? Which one and why?

522.

Is either theory (ToM and double empathy problem) dismissive of the lived autistic experience? Which one and why?

523.

Which experience matters more when it comes to understanding autism, and why?

- The lived autistic experience
- The observed autistic experience

524.

How do observed versus lived autistic experiences influence the way we conceptualize autism?

525.

If you're a medical or psychological professional, were you taught Theory of Mind, the double empathy problem, both, or neither?

526.

If you're a medical or psychological professional, does Theory of Mind, the double empathy problem, both, or neither influence your practice? Why?

527.

If you're an autistic person, how do you feel about Theory of Mind and the double empathy problem as explanations of your lived experience? Why?

528.

Have you ever asked someone if they're okay after noticing they were stimming? Why or why not?

529.

If you have asked an autistic person who prefers IFL why they have that preference:
- What was their answer?
- What did you think about their answer?
- How did you respond?
- Did their answer cause you to reflect on your preference? Why or why not?

530.

If you haven't asked an autistic person who prefers IFL why they have that preference, why haven't you?

531.

When you hear or read about PFL and IFL, what comes to mind and why?

532.

Would you change your language when speaking with an autistic person who prefers IFL? Why or why not?

533.

In order to bring about meaningful, sustainable changes, how important is it for autistic people to understand the perspectives and preferences of non-autistic people?

534.
Is autismphobia (the fear of autism, being autistic, and/or autistic characteristics) a real thing? Why or why not?

535.
Are some people actually afraid of autism? Why or why not?

536.
If some people are afraid of autism, what is the root cause of that fear? What might they be afraid of and why?

537.
What can be done to reduce any fears of autism that might exist?

538.
If you're not autistic and there were therapies available (behavioral or medication) to make you autistic, would you partake in that therapy? Why or why not?

539.
How should people decide between using identity-first language (IFL) and person-first language (PFL) when talking with or about autistic people?

- Assume PFL, but switch according to the autistic individual's preference
- Assume IFL, but switch according to the autistic individual's preference
- Always use PFL
- Always use IFL

540.

At work, what proof, if any, of autism would you require before considering a direct report's reasonable accommodation or adjustment request? Why?

541.

If you are an instructor, what messages does your training convey about neurodiversity, both implicitly and explicitly?

542.

If you're an instructor, how do you respond when differences in perspective are raised in class?

543.

Which issues important to the neurodivergent population are you most familiar with? Which issues do you feel you need to learn more about, and why?

544.

If you teach and you have "experts" come into your class to address neurodiversity, what makes them an expert?

545.

How accurate do you find the following quote, and why? "If somebody has to hide their disability to be respected, accepted, or hired, it's not their disability that's the problem, it's the judgment of it."[29]

---

[29] Quote by Julie Harris via LinkedIn. Printed with permission.

546.

What has been your favorite positive reaction from someone after telling them you or someone you love are autistic? What about the interaction makes it your favorite?

547.

If you're autistic, how often are you comfortable being your authentic neurodivergent self at work? Why?

548.

Are the words "autism" and "autistic" in and of themselves hurtful in any way to you? Why or why not?

549.

If you believe the words "autism" and "autistic" are hurtful to you, how do they bring you pain?

550.

If you believe the words "autism" and "autistic" are hurtful, how did you come to feel this way?

551.

If you believe the words "autism" and "autistic" are NOT hurtful, do they bring you happiness? Why or why not?

552.

If you believe the words "autism" and "autistic" are NOT hurtful, how did you come to feel this way?

553.

What is the most taboo autism/autistic person topic that should not be discussed? Why is that topic taboo?

554.

Why should taboo autistic topics not be discussed?

555.

Who might be harmed by discussing a taboo autistic topic? Why?

556.

How could discussing a taboo autistic topic be beneficial to autistic people?

557.

For someone who completely objects to applied behavior analysis (ABA), what benefits might they gain by listening to ABA supporters and understanding why they support it?

558.

Does understanding why people support ABA provide any useful information in advocating against ABA? Why or why not?

559.

If one were to use facts alone to advocate against ABA, how effective will they be in their anti-ABA efforts?

560.

Would ABA supporters be more or less open to listening to one's opposition to ABA if they feel their support for ABA is heard? Why or why not?

Chapter 3 Wrap-Up

Having explored the questions in this chapter, take a moment to reflect on the insights and perspectives you've encountered.

1. Three prominent themes in this chapter on talking about autism are language, autistic experiences, and differing perspectives. Consider which question(s) from this chapter would be useful for each, then write a brief script you could use to start a dialogue about these themes.

    Language:

    Autistic experiences:

    Differing perspectives:

2. Write at least three specific things you can consider changing about your worldview that would help autistic people feel included in an egalitarian society.

Chapter 4
Autism and People

"Because if someone had told me when I was younger that it was OK to not be like everybody else, that it was not my job to try to be 'normal' and to 'fit in,' that my way of seeing the world was just as valid and important as everybody else's, then I think I would have found growing up a lot easier."

~ Abigail Balfe

One of the things I appreciate about our humanity is that each person on earth is unique; no two people are exactly alike. Even identical twins have unique life experiences and perceptions that make each a wholly different person. While there are over eight billion[30] people inhabiting the earth right now and we are all different, we do have commonalities that unite us. These commonalities can be anything: global location, language, life experiences, gender, or nationality, to name a few obvious ones. Commonalities help us connect with one another because our experiences are similar. Similar experiences, in turn, enable us to empathize[31] with others in ways that could be difficult without some sort of commonality. One of the central challenges for the autistic community, given its minority status, is being viewed as "other," to the extent that finding common ground is often overlooked or even obstructed.

---

[30] According to https://www.worldometers.info/world-population/
[31] There are many definitions of empathy. The definition according to the American Psychological Association is: "Understanding a person from his or her frame of reference rather than one's own, or vicariously experiencing that person's feelings, perceptions, and thoughts."

Over the last few years since my formal identification as autistic, I've paid very close attention to how autistic and non-autistic people interact, both in mixed and homogeneous groups. When individuals or groups have something in common, such as a favorite sports team, a place they've visited, or a subject they love, I've seen barriers disappear. Challenges arise when commonalities cannot be found or when the search for them is blocked. When individuals or groups are determined to see only differences rather than commonalities, someone almost invariably becomes subjugated. I believe that all humans have sufficient commonalities from which bonds can be made. However, in some circumstances, groups, or individuals, there is minimal effort to identify commonalities and a lack of interest in doing so. I posit that this tendency contributes to the marginalization of autistic people.

To stop the marginalization of autistic people, society needs to shift its focus away from highlighting what's different about us compared to non-autistic people, and instead concentrate on the commonalities across both groups. By using our commonalities as a focal point, we will realize that we are more similar to one another than we are different. This realization will lead to significantly increased empathy, n greater sense of duty to help others with their support needs, and an overall shift towards a neurodiversity appreciation mindset. This mindset will change how we design our lives to better accommodate all neurotypes, not just those who have the most in common.[32] Everyone must see everyone else as having equal rights, regardless of differences.

In this chapter, the questions focus primarily on viewing autistic people as people rather than a collection of "symptoms" or a set of different characteristics. There is a particular emphasis on challenging our current understandings of autism across the lifespan by exploring our values, beliefs, and assumptions about these differences. While we do call out differences, critically reflect on them in light of the fact that, as humans, we are all sentient beings with similar desires to live.

---

[32] Often referred to as "neurotypical" or "neuromajority."

561.

How do parents' reactions to learning their child is autistic differ from adults' reactions to discovering they themselves are autistic?

562.

If differences exist between the reactions described in question 561, what explains these differences?

563.

How are parents' reactions to learning their child is autistic similar to adults' reactions to discovering they themselves are autistic? Why are these similarities important?

564.

If you're autistic, what is something you've accomplished that others thought you couldn't?

565.

What assumptions do people hold about how humans should interact?

566.

If you're autistic, how do you know when others sincerely appreciate you being your true autistic self?

567.

If you're autistic, how do you feel when you know others appreciate you for who you are?

568.

If you're autistic, how does feeling appreciated for being your true autistic self affect your confidence and self-worth?

569.

If you're autistic, what can people do to show you that they appreciate you for being your true autistic self? Why is this important to you?

570.

Which overlooked aspects of autism significantly impact the lives of autistic people? Why are these aspects important?

571.

Autistic people are more likely to have their lived experiences dismissed. If we accept the Centers for Disease Control's estimate of 1 in 44 children are autistic[33], then that is 1 in 44 people that have their personal experiences dismissed as inaccurate or somehow "wrong."
- How is this acceptable?
- Where is the empathy?
- Who has the power to change?
- Who has the responsibility to change?

572.

What prevents individuals from accepting that someone else's experience is valid for that person, or from making an effort to view situations from the other's perspective?

---

[33] This is a 2022 statistic obtained on the CDC website at https://www.cdc.gov/ncbddd/autism/data.html

573.

If you're autistic, have you ever been told your sensory experience was not accurate? For example, have you experienced an environment that was way too loud, but when you said something about it your experience was dismissed and/or made fun of?

- How did this make you feel?

- Why do you believe others dismissed or mocked your experience?

574.

If you're autistic, how would you like others to respond when you share your sensory experiences? Why?

575.

If you're autistic, what would you like others to know about your sensory experiences, and why?

576.

If you're autistic, do you prefer heat or cold? Why?

577.

If you're autistic, at what temperature do you start to feel uncomfortable? At what temperature does this discomfort turn to misery?

578.

If you're autistic, what sensory issues do you experience with temperature changes?

579.

If you're autistic, what do you do to prepare for attending events where there will be a lot of people?

580.

If you're autistic, how do you prevent or lessen feelings of sensory overload at events where there are a lot of people?

581.

If you're autistic, what do you do after attending an event to recover from any sensory overload you experienced?

582.

For those who are not autistic (neuromajority), do you ever feel uncomfortable interacting with an autistic person who is being their true autistic self? Why or why not?

583.

If you're not autistic and you feel uncomfortable interacting with an autistic person, what specifically about their authentic autistic self makes you uneasy? Why do you think it makes you uncomfortable?

584.

If you're not autistic and you feel uncomfortable interacting with an autistic person, is there anything autistic people could do to make you feel more comfortable interacting with them? If so, what and why?

585.

Do you believe there is such a thing as "autistic culture?" Why or why not?

586.

What does "autistic culture" mean to you?

587.

Should non-autistic people learn about autistic culture? Why or why not?

588.

What assumptions do you hold about autistic culture? Why do you hold those assumptions?

589.

If you're non-autistic, when was the last time you asked an autistic person about autistic culture? What's stopping you from asking today?

590.

What are some key features of autistic culture that differ from non-autistic culture?

591.

What's the number one rule of autistic culture? Why is it so important?

592.

Can non-autistic people be bona fide members of an autistic culture? Why or why not?

593.

What are some common misunderstandings, if any, autistic people have about how non-autistic people experience the world around them?

594.

If you're not autistic, what is one aspect of your experience of the world that you would like autistic people to understand? Why?

595.

What "problem behaviors" do non-autistic people exhibit towards autistic people? Why are they problems?

596.

Should the "problem behaviors" of non-autistics be changed with ABA interventions? Why or why not?

597.

If you were a non-autistic child, how would you feel being made to interact with others as though you were autistic? Why?

598.

If you're autistic, what's something that makes you feel great about yourself? Why does it make you great?

599.

If you're autistic, which of these two things is more frustrating for you?
- Being autistic
- Not being understood by non-autistics

600.

How does being autistic impact your ability to vote in an election?

601.

If you're autistic and have challenges getting out to vote in person, does your location allow you to vote by mail-in ballot or absentee vote? Why or why not?

602.

If you're autistic and have challenges voting, what would help you reduce those challenges? Why would these help?

603.

What can lawmakers and election personnel do to support autistic people's voting efforts?

604.

If you're autistic, what was something a non-autistic person said to you that made you think, "Wow! They understand me!" afterwards?

604.

If you're autistic, what is one of the best questions someone has ever asked you about your autistic experiences? How did the person respond to your answer? How did their question make you feel?

605.

If you're autistic, what are some things that you do not like about waiting rooms, especially at a doctor's office? Why?

606.

What changes could be made to waiting rooms to better accommodate the needs of autistics?

607.
What are ways you've successfully reduced your discomfort while in a waiting room?

608.
What are the similarities and differences in the experiences of autistic children and autism parents[34]?

609.
How might embracing "autism parent" as an identity fit into the neurodiversity paradigm? Why?

610.
Why do some people view the term "autism parent" as appropriating their child's autism for their own identity rather than as a separate, unique identity?

611.
What are the similarities and differences between transgender rights issues and autistic rights issues?

612.
Why do transgendered people have to fight for their rights to live their lives as they see fit rather than how others see fit?

613.
Why do autistic people have to fight for their rights to live their lives as they see fit rather than how others see fit?

---

[34] An "autism parent" is the parent of an autistic child, but is who is not autistic themselves.

614.
If you are both transgender and autistic, what unique challenges do you face that you might not face if you were either transgender or autistic, but not both?

615.
In what ways are transgender rights and autistic rights human rights? Are there ways in which they are not human rights?

616.
Are transgender rights issues and autistic rights issues more similar or more different from each other? Why?

617.
Do you like eating leftovers? Why or why not?

618.
Are autistic people held to a different standard when it comes to interacting with others (of any neurotype) as compared to non-autistic people? Why or why not?

619.
If you believe there are different standards for autistic and non-autistic people when it comes to interacting with others, what standards differ and why do they differ?

620.
Are autistic people across all levels of support needs capable of experiencing emotions and demonstrating traits such as passion, compassion, humor, generosity, kindness, and personal style? Why or why not?

621.

If you're autistic, which type of microaggression[35] have you experienced most frequently?
- Microassaults (involve explicit and intentional derogation)
- Microinsults (involve rudeness or insensitivity towards another's heritage or identity)
- Microinvalidations (occur when the thoughts and feelings of a minority group member seem to be excluded, negated, or nullified as a result of their minority status)

622.

What stereotypes and stigmas about interacting with non-autistic people persist among autistic people? Why do these perceptions continue?

623.

What stereotypes and stigmas about interacting with autistic people persist among non-autistic people? Why do these perceptions continue?

624.

Do autistic people *enjoy* interacting with non-autistic people? How do you know?

625.

If autistic people don't enjoy interacting with non-autistic people, why is this the case? How do you know?

---

[35] Sue, D. W., Capodilupo, C. M., Torino, G. C., Bucceri, J. M., Holder, A. M. B., Nadal, K. L., & Esquilin, M. (2007). Racial microaggressions in everyday life: Implications for practice. *American Psychologist, 62*(4), 271-286. doi: 10.1037/0003-066X.62.4.271

626.

Do non-autistic people *enjoy* interacting with autistic people? How do you know?

627.

If non-autistic people don't enjoy interacting with autistic people, why is this the case? How do you know?

628.

Should anyone holding an elected office overseeing autistic services strategy at a national level (such as a Minister of Autism) be autistic? Why or why not?

629.

What are the advantages and disadvantages of being autistic as an elected official overseeing autistic services strategy at a national level?

630.

What are the advantages and disadvantages of being non-autistic as an elected official overseeing autistic services strategy at a national level?

631.

What message is sent to the autistic community if an elected official overseeing the autistic services strategy at a national level is not autistic?

632.

What should autistic people understand about the interactions between autistic and non-autistic people? Why is this knowledge important?

633.
How do the people around an autistic person contribute to building that person's confidence? Why is this important?

634.
How much of the responsibility for confidence-building falls exclusively on the autistic person?

635.
Assuming the person has the desired qualifications and experience, would you vote for a candidate for elected office who is openly autistic? Why or why not?

636.
Would the office for which an autistic person is running for make a difference in your decision to vote or not vote for them? Why or why not?

637.
What concerns, if any, would you have about an autistic person in an elected position? Why?

638.
All other things being equal, would an autistic person or a non-autistic person make a better elected official? Why?

639.
If you had a chance to speak directly with a high-ranking elected official in the federal government, what three specific issues related to autism, autistic culture, or the lives of autistic people would you prioritize in your discussion?

640.

What is one specific thing would you *ask* of an elected official in their official capacity regarding autism?

641.

After being evaluated for autism, how might parents react upon learning their child is *not* autistic?

642.

In the autistic context, what does "warrior parent" mean to you? Why?

643.

Do you perceive being a "warrior parent" as a positive, negative, or neutral thing? Why?

644.

Do warrior parents exist for the entire range of how autism is expressed? Why or why not?

645.

Does being a "warrior parent" mean the parent is waging a war against autism? If so, who or what is the enemy? What weapons are used to wage this war?

646.

How can you tell when a non-speaking autistic person's emotional state improves or worsens? What do you look for?

647.

In what ways do non-speaking autistic people communicate their emotional state to you?

648.

In what ways do you communicate with non-speaking autistic people?

649.

Are you able to understand what non-speaking individuals are thinking? If so, how?

650.

If you can identify changes in the emotional states of non-speaking autistic people, how long did it take you to learn to recognize their emotions? What helped you learn this?

651.

If you're autistic, what's *your* profound, thought-provoking insight about being autistic in a world not made for autistics?

652.

Is there a universal commonality shared among the infinitely varied autistic experiences? Why or why not?

653.

What commonalities exist between autistic people who have significant support needs and possibly co-occurring conditions[36], and non-autistic people who have minimal support needs and no co-occurring conditions?

654.

What are some of the challenges a person may experience as one who supports an autistic family member?

655.

How has supporting an autistic family member positively or negatively impacted your life?

656.

If you support an autistic person, what support do *you* need?

657.

Acknowledging that there are ups and downs, is supporting your autistic family member a rewarding experience or a burdensome experience? Why or why not?

658.

If you support an autistic person, what perspectives do you hold about other autistic people who may have greater or lesser support needs than the person you support?

---

[36] Since writing this question, I have changed my perspective on "co-occurring conditions." I do not consider autism as a condition. I consider autism as one of many ways neurology can exist and as such, other things cannot "co-occur" with it, by definition.

659.

What are three things you want the world to know about supporting autistic people?

660.

Has the autistic community inadvertently created fears that deter non-autistic people from engaging in conversation with autistic people? If so, what are these fears and why do they exist?

661.

Could autistic people be perceived as being unreasonable and angry?

662.

Is social isolation more of an issue for the autistic person or non-autistic person? Why?

663.

Is stimming more of an issue for the autistic person or non-autistic person? Why?

664.

If stimming is an issue in social interactions, what resolutions would you suggest and why? Who benefits from the resolutions?

665.

If you're a medical provider and learned that a patient-to-be is autistic, what would you do differently as you interact with the patient (if anything)? Why?

666.

What's something you are thankful for as a result of being identified as autistic? Why?

667.

What is something you want others to know about your experience in supporting or raising an autistic child?

668.

If you're autistic, which is more important to you when interacting with non-autistic people:

- Learning to communicate their way
- Helping them understand socially acceptable behaviors from the autistic perspective

Why did you choose your answer?

669.

If you selected "Learning to communicate their way" in question 668, what are your views about "Helping them understand socially acceptable behaviors from the autistic perspective"? Why?

670.

If you selected "Helping them understand socially acceptable behaviors from the autistic perspective" in question 668, what are your views about "Learning to communicate their way"? Why?

671.

What are some misconceptions about parents of autistic children that you find frustrating?

672.

What advice would you give to parents of autistic children who are overwhelmed and frustrated by the conflicting information and misunderstandings about autism? Why is this advice important?

673.

What questions would you ask autistic adults to gain insights about being an autistic child?

674.

How can autistic advocates help you? What would you like them to do differently?

675.

If you are a parent of an autistic child, do you feel like your voice is heard by the autistic community? Why or why not?

676.

What are your feelings about "Autism Acceptance Month?"

677.

If you're autistic, do you ever feel exploited during Autism Acceptance Month (or any other month, for that matter)? Why or why not?

678.

What do you perceive are the top three things autistic people do or experience that cause difficulties for non-autistic people? Why do you think these are challenging for non-autistic people?

679.

Have you personally experienced difficulties as a result of interacting with autistic people? Describe that interaction and why it was difficult for you.

680.

April 2nd is known as Autism Acceptance Day. Whether or not you are autistic, what does today mean to you? Why?

681.

If you're not autistic, what do you hope recognition on April 2nd will do for autistic people? Why?

682.

If you're autistic, what would you like the world to know about Autism Acceptance Day, and why?

683.

If you are a parent of a non-autistic child, would you consider using ABA to increase "helpful behaviors" or decrease "harmful behaviors"? Why or why not?

684.

Are "social norms" the same construct as "socially acceptable?" Why or why not?

Chapter 4 Wrap-Up

Now that you've read through the questions in this chapter, take a moment to reflect the journey thus far.

1. How have the questions about autistic people made you reflect on what autism means?

2. Which questions would you ask an autistic person regarding their experience being autistic and why? Flip back through the chapter and note the question number as part of your response.

3. After reading this chapter, how might you interact with autistic people differently?

4. What should be society's primary concern when it comes to how we think about autistic people? Why?

Chapter 5
Social Interactions

"If we could look into each other's hearts and understand the unique challenges each of us faces, I think we would treat each other much more gently, with more love, patience, tolerance, and care."

~ Marvin J. Ashton

Newton's third law of motion states that for every action, there is an equal and opposite reaction; this means that in every interaction, a pair of forces acts on the two interacting objects. The forces are equal in magnitude and opposite in direction, always occurring in pairs[37]. This principle can be metaphorically applied to our understanding of autism, the autistic community, and individual autistic people. Just as forces influence objects, societal values, beliefs, and assumptions about autism inevitably impact autistic individuals. Whether directly or indirectly, every action related to how autism is conceptualized or talked about triggers a reaction that affects those within the autistic community.

The Pyramid of Effects

"Meltdown", "on the spectrum", "deficits", "high functioning"—our understanding of autism is shaped by our underlying values, beliefs, and

---

[37] The Physics Classroom. (2022). Lesson 4—Newton's third law of motion. https://www.physicsclassroom.com/class/newtlaws/Lesson-4/Newton-s-Third-Law

assumptions. The Pyramid of Effects illustrates this complex relationship, demonstrating how these foundational elements not only frame how we conceptualize autism and autistics, but also influence the ways in which we interact with autistics and affect their self-worth. The model highlights a bidirectional series of relationships, with each level influencing those adjacent to it, such that changes at any level can have both direct and indirect impacts that extend beyond their immediate effects. Thus, while a change may seem insignificant in the moment, it could have profound effects up and down the levels. This chapter highlights this concept and offers questions to reflect on how your own values, beliefs, and assumptions shape your concepts of autism and the autistic world.

Values, Beliefs, and Assumptions

Our values, beliefs, and assumptions quietly steer the course of our lives, often without us realizing their profound influence. What we cherish and hold important—be it principles, objects, or people—become guiding stars in our decision-making processes, illuminating what we deem worthy or useful in some way. Our beliefs, which are those truths we hold unquestionable, shape how we view the world and the lens through which we interpret our experiences. Together, our values and beliefs construct the assumptions by which we operate. These assumptions are the expectations we bank on without proof and the unseen rules we follow. This often-unseen framework not only shapes our personal narratives but also impacts others around us in significant ways.[38]

---

[38] Janeski, P. (N.D.). *Values, beliefs and assumptions*. https://pauljaneski.com/beliefs-values-assumptions/.

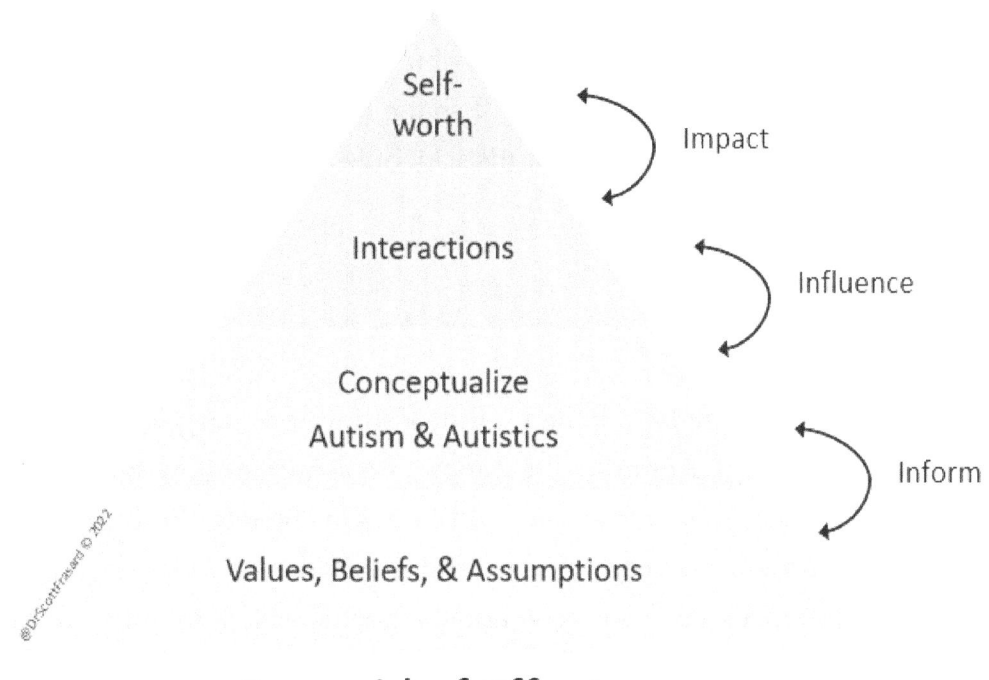

Pyramid of Effects

- Self-worth ← Impact
- Interactions ← Influence
- Conceptualize Autism & Autistics ← Inform
- Values, Beliefs, & Assumptions

Conceptualizing Autism and Autistics

How we see everything around us is rooted in our values, beliefs, and assumptions. Take these two different people for example: one, who was raised to believe that coffee is unhealthy, and another, who was raised to believe coffee is beneficial and energizing. The former person would be more likely to avoid coffee at breakfast or during work breaks, whereas the latter might regularly enjoy a cup. The values, beliefs, and assumptions developed over time in each of these two people shaped how they view coffee and its consumption. Thus, how they conceptualize, act towards, and behave around coffee is a result of their values, beliefs, and assumptions.

The same thing happens in all aspects of our lives. As Clifton et al. note[39], "A half-century of research clearly indicates that various beliefs shape behavior and wellbeing" (p. 83). If we view autistic people as lesser than non-autistic people—such as in competence, capability to contribute to society, and the ability to live independently—then this perception will shape how we define them as people. It will also affect how we interact with autistic people and the autistic community.

Interactions

Given that our values, beliefs, and assumptions largely shape how we conceptualize the world around us, it stands to reason that how we conceptualize the world determines how we interact within it. Our beliefs about people and the world can affect how we perceive, judge, and respond to the situations and people we encounter. For instance, if we view autistic people as less intelligent or capable, we might dismiss their ideas or be hesitant to collaborate with them. This bias can skew our communication and how we interpret their actions, often resulting in misunderstandings and hindering the development of meaningful connections. Conversely, if our values emphasize compassion and empathy, we are more likely to engage autistic people understandingly and respectfully. This approach would then foster a search for common ground and efforts to bridge gaps in communication or understanding.

While our values, beliefs, and assumptions greatly influence our attitudes towards others, they are not set in stone. They can evolve over time, shaped by new experiences and exposures to different ideas and people. Acknowledging and

---

[39] Clifton, J. D. W., Baker, J. D, Yaden, D. B., Paolo, T., Zeng, G., Schwartz, H. A., Park, C. L., Clifton, A. B. W., Miller, J. L., Giorgi, S., & Seligman, M. E. P. (2019). Primal world beliefs. *Psychological Assessment, 31*(1), 82-99. doi: 10.1037/pas0000639

challenging our biases is essential for fostering open-mindedness and a willingness to learn from diverse perspectives. In doing so, we not only improve our interactions with autistic people, but also contribute to building their positive self-worth and creating a more inclusive society.

Self-worth

Self-worth refers to the value and regard we have for ourselves. People often have an inherent need to feel valuable and worthy. This need for self-worth is often tied to how individuals evaluate themselves in relation to their own standards and is influenced by their experiences, relationships, and interactions with others. When people feel like they are meeting others' expectations of who they should be, their sense of self-worth is likely to be high. Conversely, when they feel like they are falling short of these expectations, their sense of self-worth is likely to be low.

Interactions with others can have both positive and negative effects on self-worth. Positive interactions, such as compliments, encouragement, and validation, can boost someone's self-worth. These interactions communicate that the other person is valued, respected, and appreciated. Conversely, negative interactions, such as criticism, rejection, and disrespect, can lower someone's self-worth. When someone feels devalued or disrespected, they are more likely to have negative feelings about themselves. This also impacts how we interact with one another and this interaction is bidirectional.

Bidirectionality

The cause-and-effect chain described above also happens in the opposite direction for the same reasons. When an autistic person has positive self-worth as a result of their interactions with others, they perceive their interactions with others in a better light. They also tend to have a more positive impact on those interactions, which in turn influences others' conceptualizations of both autistic people and autism. With a more positive conceptualization of autistic people and autism as a whole, others' values, beliefs, and assumptions about autistic people and autism take on a more positive perspective. Therefore, it is crucial to recognize that every interaction with autistic people simultaneously affects both autistic and non-autistic individuals.

In this chapter, the questions focus primarily on how we interact with one another, with a focus on changing perspectives for everyone's benefit.

685.
If the majority of humanity communicated nonverbally and only a small minority used spoken words, would the non-speaking majority attempt to stop the speaking minority from speaking? Why or why not?

686.
What assumptions do we have about spoken communication?

687.
In the United States, should laws and insurance regulations mandate support for autistic people that does not rely on behaviorism-based methods and prohibit those that do?

688.
What are the advantages and disadvantages of requiring non-behaviorism-based support methods and banning behaviorism-based support methods?

689.
You arrive at your polling precinct to vote on election day. On the ballot is a proposition to ban all forms of applied behavior analysis (ABA), to include any therapies based on behaviorism. Would you vote for or against the proposition? Why?

690.
If ABA was banned, would anyone benefit? Who and why?

691.
If ABA was banned, would anyone be harmed? Who and why?

692.

Is it unprofessional for an employee to use sensory aids, such as a squishy fidget toy or ear defenders, during a high-profile meeting with corporate executives? Why or why not?

693.

Would your response to question 692 differ if the employee were autistic? Why or why not?

694.

If an employee requires a sensory aid, would you discourage or prevent them from attending high-profile meetings with executives? Why or why not?

695.

What assumptions do people have about others who need sensory support devices at work?

696.

Would your perspective of someone who needs sensory support devices at work differ if the person was in an executive position versus an entry-level position? Why or why not?

697.

What purposes does masking[40] serve for non-autistic (neuromajority) people, if any? Why or why not?

---

[40] Masking in the autistic context refers to the strategies autistic individuals use to mimic, suppress, or alter their natural behaviors and responses to conform to social norms and avoid negative judgments.

698.
If you are non-autistic (neuromajority), have you ever felt compelled to mask when in the presence of autistic people in order to feel that you fit in? What was the situation?

699.
If you are non-autistic (neuromajority), have you felt compelled to mask when in the presence of other non-autistic people? Why or why not?

700.
Is it acceptable for an autistic person to say something that ends up making a non-autistic person very uncomfortable? Why or why not?

701.
If it's acceptable for an autistic person to say something that makes a non-autistic person very uncomfortable, what assumptions might be held about the intent of the autistic person's statement?

702.
If it isn't acceptable for an autistic person to say something that makes a non-autistic person very uncomfortable, what assumptions might be held about the intent of the autistic person's statement?

703.
If an autistic person says something that ends up making a non-autistic person very uncomfortable, assuming what the autistic person said was factual and was not out of context, why might the non-autistic person feel very uncomfortable?

704.
If you were a manager in a large, multinational organization, would you promote a highly skilled employee, who works well with other employees, communicates well, has everyone's respect, but is a non-speaking autistic person, to a supervisor position? Why or why not?

705.
What concerns, if any, would you have with a person described in question 704 in a supervisor role? Why?

706.
If you were the manager of the employee described in question 704, how would you help that person be successful in their new position of supervisor?

707.
Referring back to question 704, would the size of the team to be led influence your decision to promote the person? Why or why not?

708.
If you are not an autistic person, have you ever been made to feel you do not matter simply because you're not autistic?

709.
If you have been made to feel you do not matter simply because you're not autistic, what is an example of this happening to you?

710.
Without identifying specific people, who has made you feel that you don't matter simply because you are not autistic?

711.

If you are an autistic person, have you ever been made to feel you do not matter simply because you are autistic? Why or why not?

712.

If you've ever been made to feel you do not matter simply because you are autistic, what is an example of this happening to you?

713.

Without identifying specific people, who has made you feel that you do not matter simply because you are autistic?

714.

If you have not felt that you do not matter simply because you are autistic, why do you think you have not experienced this?

715.

Generally speaking, does a power struggle exist between the autistic community and the non-autistic community?

716.

If there is a power struggle between the autistic and non-autistic communities, what is the struggle over? Why does the struggle exist?

717.

If a power struggle exists between the autistic and non-autistic communities, describe the power dynamic.

718.
If a power struggle exists between the autistic and non-autistic communities, how can the struggle be reduced or eliminated?

719.
Assuming it exists, does the power differential between autistic and non-autistic communities appear different depending on the community to which one belongs? Why or why not?

720.
Is there an appropriate amount of time it should take a person to respond to another during a verbal conversation for the response to be considered "correct?" Why or why not?

721.
Should individuals be taught how long they have to respond if they don't reply within a certain amount of time during a verbal conversation? Why or why not?

722.
Is the response time for autistic people treated differently than non-autistic people? Why or why not?

723.
Are there social norms regarding how long one has to respond to another during a verbal conversation? What about during a non-verbal conversation? Why or why not?

724.
Do autistic children have the right to *not* communicate with spoken words? Why or why not?

725.
If autistic children are able to communicate without speaking words, is that good enough? Why or why not?

726.
If autistic children have the right to communicate without spoken words, do autistic adults have the right to communicate without spoken words as well? Why or why not?

727.
Does anyone question whether or not non-autistic children or adults have the right to communicate without spoken words? Why or why not?

728.
If you function in a training capacity at work and teach new employees as they enter the organization, how would you respond upon learning one of your learners is autistic?

729.
What actions would you take to welcome a new autistic member to an organization?

730.
What actions would you take to help a new autistic member learn what they need to know about an organization?

731.
What assumptions would you hold about a new autistic employee's ability to do the job for which they were hired? Why?

732.
What emotion do you most frequently experience?

733.
What physical sensations or feelings typically accompany the emotion you identified in question 732?

734.
Along with the primary emotion you identified in question 732, do you experience any other emotions in conjunction with this one? If so, which?

735.
How do you feel when your emotion from question 732 subsides?

736.
What would you like others to know about your experience with this emotion from question 732?

737.
Without debating the pros and cons of universal basic income (UBI), how might universal basic supports (UBS) work?

738.
What policies would need to be in place for UBS to provide positive impacts?

739.

How would UBS affect the lives of autistic people, whether formally diagnosed, self-identified, or not identified?

740.

How would UBS impact the lives of all people, not just autistic people?

741.

Is masking, as it pertains to autistic people, an adaptive or maladaptive behavior? Why or why not?

742.

If you consider masking to be an adaptive behavior, what assumptions are you making about autistic people who engage in masking?

743.

If you consider masking to be a maladaptive behavior, what assumptions are you making about autistic people who engage in masking?

744.

If you consider masking to be an adaptive behavior, what does this imply about the environment in which the autistic person exists?

745.

If you consider masking to be a maladaptive behavior, what does this imply about the environment in which the autistic person exists?

746.

Is masking a behavior or a response? Why?

747.
These days, we see a lot of talk about organizations embracing neurodiversity. Frequently the phrase "competitive advantage" appears in connection with hiring neurodivergent people. If you are neurodivergent, how does this make you feel?

748.
If you're neurodivergent and an organization claims that having you as an employee is a competitive advantage, would you feel supported or exploited? Why?

749.
Whose interests are organizations serving when they consider hiring neurodivergent people as a competitive advantage? Why?

750.
What should organization leaders consider when creating and implementing a strategy that leverages neurodiversity as a competitive advantage? Why are these considerations important?

751.
If an organization's purpose for a neurodiversity as a competitive advantage strategy is to benefit both the organization and the neurodivergent employees, which motivation comes first? Why?

752.
Imagine a world where everyone, across all languages and cultures, communicated explicitly. What would happen if, starting tomorrow, people only used clear, direct language instead of hinting or implying their needs?

753.

In a world where everybody only communicated explicitly, would autistic people have fewer or more communication issues? Why?

754.

In a world where everybody only communicated explicitly, would non-autistic people have fewer or more communication issues? Why?

755.

How could dialogue between people of different neurotypes change in a world where everybody only communicated explicitly? Why?

756.

How do you react when you hear autistic ways of being referred to as "symptoms"?

757.

Does it matter what we call autistic differences, such as the unique ways autistics sense the world, communicate, and express themselves? Why or why not?

758.

If you feel "symptoms" is an accurate descriptor for autistic differences, why do you feel this way?

759.

If you feel "symptoms" is not an accurate descriptor for autistic differences, why do you feel this way?

760.

What assumptions do people have about spoken communication? Why do people have these assumptions?

761.

How do parents' reactions to learning their child is autistic differ from adults' reactions to discovering they themselves are autistic?

762.

If there is a difference in the reactions of parents learning their child is autistic compared to autistic adults discovering their own autism, what might explain this difference?

763.

How are parents' reactions to learning their child is autistic similar to adults' reactions to discovering they themselves are autistic? Why?

764.

What are the advantages and disadvantages of prioritizing non-behaviorism-based support methods over those based on behaviorism?

765.

What are some neurodiversity-affirming responses to take when an autistic person has a meltdown at work? Why are these responses important?

766.

What assumptions do people have about an adult experiencing a meltdown?

767.
Should there be any "blame" assigned when an adult has a meltdown at work? Why or why not?

768.
How should a supervisor respond if an autistic employee were to have a meltdown at work? Why?

769.
Would the response to an autistic employee having a meltdown differ based on the employee's role within the organization's hierarchy, such as entry-level versus director? Why or why not?

770.
How can organizations and interviewers change their interview processes to be neurodiversity-affirming?

771.
When is being indirect the most appropriate communication approach? Why is this approach beneficial?

772.
When is being direct the most appropriate communication approach? Why is this approach beneficial?

773.
How often should people use indirect communication in lieu of direct communication? Why?

774.
What should instructors know about the positive or negative experience of autistic individuals trying to learn? Why are these experiences important?

775.
What are some actions instructors take in the classroom setting that can make learning difficult for autistic people? How about in live, online learning situations? In asynchronous online learning situations?

776.
As the world becomes more accepting of remote work, is this an advantage or disadvantage for autistic workers? Why or why not?

777.
Are diversity, equality, and inclusion (DEI) efforts more inclusive of neurodivergent employees and potential employees, or do they fall short of their intended purpose? What factors contribute to their success or limitations?

From your own personal experiences, do you feel that diversity, equality, and inclusion (DEI) efforts are more inclusive of neurodivergent employees/potential employees or do they fall short of their intended purpose? Why or why not?

778.
How can organizations better support the executive functioning challenges autistic employees may experience at work?

779.

When an autistic professional has executive functioning issues, should they:
- Take the day off?
- Work through the fog?
- Go to work, but do "easy work?"
- Something else?

780.

What perceptions do you have of someone who decides not to work one day because of executive functioning issues? What assumptions drive these perceptions?

781.

If you were a supervisor, how would you handle an employee's unplanned time off request (e.g., "calling in sick") when it's due to the employee experiencing executive functioning difficulties? Why?

782.

How would you feel if your colleague, with whom you are working on a high-priority, high-visibility project due soon, called out sick due to experiencing executive functioning issues? Why would you feel this way?

783.

Is there a moral obligation to adjust a design (e.g., a store's layout and features) to ensure inclusivity when the original design excludes some people? Why or why not?

784.
What is an example of an exclusionary practice or situation that could be made more inclusive, yet is often considered impossible or nearly impossible to change?

785.
When creating policies for autism support (such as resources provided, insurance coverage, curricula, licensing, etc.,), which perspective is most valuable for making informed decisions about the support needs of autistic people?

- First-hand perspectives from actually autistic individuals
- Second-hand perspectives from non-autistic caregivers of autistic people
- Academic or researcher perspectives
- Psychological professional perspectives

Why did you choose that answer?

786.
Other than the options noted in question 785, are there other autism support perspectives you feel should be given significant consideration? Why or why not?

787.
Of the autism support perspectives noted in question 785, are there any perspectives that you feel are completely irrelevant? Why or why not?

788.
Should all states have a governing body that licenses and oversees ABA practice? Why or why not?

789.

What are the potential consequences of implementing oversight for ABA practices?

790.

What are the potential consequences of *not* implementing oversight for ABA practice?

791.

In the states that do not require licensure or have a regulatory system for ABA, how does one file and address grievances and affect change?

792.

As of 2023, there were 18 states that had no governing body nor licensing requirements for ABA practitioners[41]. Is this acceptable?

793.

What is the connection between talking and communication?

794.

If everyone on earth suddenly adopted a new perspective on equality tomorrow, how would the world change? Why?

795.

How does inequality among humans make humanity worse?

796.

How does inequality among humans make humanity better?

---

[41] AppliedBehaviorAnalysisEdu.org. (2023). *Applied behavior analysis licensing laws and practice requirements by state.*

797.

Is it inevitable that inequality will exist? Why or why not?

798.

What, if any, are the downsides to equality?

799.

How would having full equality among all humans change policy, politics, services, priorities, etc.?

800.

What are your perceptions and experiences with people who communicate very directly? Do autistic and non-autistic people perceive and experience this kind of directness differently?

801.

Does direct communication make you feel uncomfortable? Why or why not?

802.

How do you interpret being asked questions about something you believe you have already clearly articulated?

803.

What should autistic people know about direct communication?

804.

Does communicating directly erode the intended message?

805.

Should people avoid being direct in their communication whenever possible?

806.

What frustrations, if any, do you feel when someone is being direct?

807.

Is there a line between being direct and being "too direct?" If so, what is that line?

808.

What is the relationship between cognitive processes and behaviors?

809.

Are our cognitive processes different for learned behaviors as compared to conditioned behaviors?

810.

What role does instinct play in our behaviors?

811.

A coworker frequently questions your instructions and asks for clarifications, often commenting, "That doesn't make any sense to me." They also sometimes challenge your re-explanations with remarks like, "But that's not what you just said."

How would you characterize this person's responses, not knowing anything else than what's included above?

812.

With comments like the ones described in question 811, do you assume a positive or negative intent? How would you respond to the coworker described in question

813.

Would your reaction to the situation described in question 811 differ if these comments occurred during private one-on-one conversations versus in group settings? Why or why not?

814.

Would your opinion or characterization of the coworker in question 811 change if you had more information about them and the situation? If so, what additional information would you need?

815.

How would the comments described in question 811 make you feel as the giver of the instructions? Why?

816.

If a coworker continued making the kinds of comments described in question 811, should they be subject to disciplinary measures? Why or why not?

817.

Are there any situations where such comments described in question 811 would be welcomed and encouraged? Describe those situations.

818.

Should individuals who think, act, or communicate differently from the majority be compelled to suppress their natural tendencies to conform to others? Why or why not?

819.

What is the most appropriate approach for bridging communication gaps between neurodivergent and neurotypical individuals?

820.

Is direct eye contact necessary for effective communication? Why or why not?

Chapter 5 Wrap-Up

Now that you've explored the questions in this chapter, pause for a moment to consider the insights you've gained.

1. Which five questions would help you approach interactions with autistic people differently? Note the question number as part of your response.

2. For each of the five questions you noted above, how might each change the way you interact with autistic people? Describe an interaction with an autistic person using one of these questions.

3. Take some time to have at least one interaction with an autistic person as described above. How did this interaction make you feel? What difference do you think it made?

Chapter 6
Autism, Support, and Services

"Everyone is struggling. I suppose we must try to understand and learn rather than judge."

~ Amish Tripathi

It is not enough to merely change how we think about autism, autistic people, and how we help them navigate a non-autistic world. We must think more broadly and question everything we currently understand about autism. Not only will this provide a positive impact on the autistic community, but it will also yield enormous gains for all humanity.

It is essential to approach autism and autism-related issues with an open mind, a willingness to learn, and a non-judgmental attitude. This is especially important when it comes to providing support and services to autistic individuals. Historically, support and services for autistic people have been based on the assumption that autism is a deficit that needs to be remedied or cured. This approach has often focused on teaching autistic individuals to conform to societal norms and expectations, rather than celebrating their unique strengths and talents.

Having come from a helping industry myself (emergency medical services), I have a certain idea of what support means. Over the past year of asking reflective questions to ponder, I've challenged my own ideas of what it means to help not only autistic people, but people in general. My initial thoughts about supporting the autistic community changed so much that I ended up writing an entire chapter in this book about rethinking support for all (see Chapter 10: Rethinking Support, Disability, and Advocacy).

In this chapter, the questions explore our conceptualizations of autism and the implications these have for support and services for autistic individuals. The questions are designed to challenge your perceptions of available support services and their utility for autistic people. As you read through this chapter, imagine the possibilities for the future, free from today's constraints imposed by political, economic, and philosophical realities.

821.

If an autistic person receives support for help in their day-to-day needs at work, do they have an unfair advantage over their colleagues? Why or why not?

822.

If you feel that providing support gives autistic employees an unfair advantage, what specific advantage do you perceive? Why do you consider it unfair?

823.

How can we help autistic people so that they thrive with passion, compassion, humor, style, generosity, and kindness, regardless of their level of support needs?

824.

What stops people from helping autistic people thrive? Why do these barriers exist?

825.

If you were formally identified as autistic in adulthood, was applied behavior analysis (ABA) recommended to you as a treatment or therapy?

826.

If you were formally identified as autistic as an adult and ABA was recommended, was there an explanation as to why?

827.

If you were formally identified as autistic in adulthood and ABA was *not* recommended, was there an explanation as to why?

828.

At what age is ABA no longer recommended? Why?

829.

If you once opposed ABA as a means to treat autistic people but now support its use, what caused you to change your mind? Why?

830.

If you support ABA, why do you support its use?

831.

What would you say to an autistic person who opposes ABA and views it as abusive? Why?

832.

If you support ABA, what could lead you to feeling defensive in conversations meant to share perspectives and foster dialogue?

833.

Do you consider autistic people who actively oppose ABA as being troublemakers? Why or why not?

834.

If you believe speaking out against ABA makes one a troublemaker, for whom do they make trouble?

835.

If you believe speaking out against ABA makes one a troublemaker, is the trouble they make a good thing or a bad thing? Why?

836.

Who do you see opposing ABA more frequently—autistic people or non-autistic people? Why?

837.

Hypothetically, if the resources and distribution channels exist to meet all conceivable support needs of autistic people, what would prevent decision-makers from changing legislation, policies, and practices to make these supports available to all who need them?

838.

Who controls the resources meant to support autistic people? Why do they have this control?

839.

Who controls the narrative regarding the availability of support resources? Why do they control this narrative?

840.

Are support resources actually scarce? If so, which ones and why?

841.

If there were enough support resources for all autistic people who want or need them, would there still be a need to categorize people by levels or degrees of severity to prioritize supports? Why or why not?

842.

If sufficient support resources were not available for all autistic people who want or need them, who should receive support and who should go without? Why?

843.
Do an autistic person's support needs indicate how well they function in society? Why or why not?

844.
Which is more helpful to an autistic person: functional labels or specifically stated support needs? Why?

845.
If specifically stated support needs are more useful than functional labels, why do people still use functional labels to speak of autistic people?

846.
Are "support needs" and "understanding needs" the same, different, or is one a subset of the other? Why?

847.
Can ABA be effectively used to teach English to someone fluent in another language? Why or why not?

848.
If ABA can help someone speak a foreign language, does it also ensure they understand the meanings of the words they use? Why or why not?

849.
What contributions, if any, could ABA make in helping someone learn to speak a foreign language? How would it help?

850.
What is the relationship between learned helplessness and compliance?

851.
Does ABA leverage or encourage learned helplessness to achieve compliance, and if so, how might this affect the sense of self among autistic people receiving ABA?

852.
Does the marketing of ABA contribute to a cycle of learned helplessness among parents of autistic children, leading them to depend solely on ABA and exclude other options?

853.
Do parents of autistic children enrolled in ABA experience learned helplessness as a result of ABA? Why or why not?

854.
Is there anything inherently unhealthy about autism in and of itself? Why or why not?

855.
If you believe there is something inherently unhealthy about autism, what assumptions do you hold that lead you to this belief?

856.
If you believe there is something unhealthy about autism, what would help an autistic person be healthier?

857.

If ABA can be used to teach autistic people how to interact with non-autistic people, could it also be used to teach non-autistic people how to interact with autistic people? Why or why not?

858.

What assumptions about autistic behavior would lead some to think that behavioral intervention is necessary? Why?

859.

When it comes to supporting autistic people, which of the following is the most important to consider:
- Outwardly observed behaviors or traits
- The autistic person's lived experiences
- How the autistic person's behavior affects others
- Something else

Why did you select your answer?

860.

If you consider outwardly observed behaviors or traits as the most important factor from question 859, what underlying assumptions about autism and autistic people lead you to this choice?

861.

If you consider an autistic person's lived experiences as the most important factor from question 859, what underlying assumptions about autism and autistic people lead you to this choice?

862.
In the dialogue regarding support needs for autistic people, do we lose sight of *specific* support needs for autistic individuals?

863.
Do conversations about support needs often overlook specific types of necessary support, and is this oversight intentional? If so, why does it occur?

864.
What would change in the discussion about support if we replaced the general term "support needs" with specific references to the exact types of necessary supports? Why would this change?

865.
How would legislation, regulations, and policies change if specific supports were referenced rather than referring to them in generalities?

866.
If support needs were spoken about with more specificity, would how we talk about autism in general change?

867.
When deciding who receives which supports, which approach is more effective: categorizing people or identifying specific support needs? Why?

868.
Is it necessary to categorize autistic people into different groups in order to provide support services equitably? Why or why not?

869.

Who benefits from the current approach to providing support services to autistic people? Why do they benefit?

870.

Could we adopt a one-for-one need-support service approach[42] to better assist the autistic community, assuming there is a willingness to change relevant laws, regulations, and policies? Why or why not?

871.

If someone has a specific support need, should it matter if someone is autistic or not? Why or why not?

872.

If supports were predicated on actual needs versus perceived needs associated with a diagnosis, how would that change the concept of autism?

873.

If you're autistic, have you ever been denied support because another person self-identified as autistic? If so, what specific support were you denied?

874.

Was the support you were denied, as mentioned in question 873, specifically redirected to the other person who self-identified as autistic? If so, why was redirected, and how did you verify this?

---

[42] In my mind, a one-to-one need-support service approach prioritizes individuals' specific needs over categorical diagnoses based on a medical model. For instance, an autistic person who needs support with daily grooming would receive support for this activity of daily living based on their need and regardless of their autism diagnosis. Thus, support services would be identity agnostic and tailored to specific needs.

875.

Regarding question 873, did you verify whether or not the other person was autistic? If so, how?

876.

Regarding question 873, is it possible that the support given to the other person (in lieu of you) was unrelated to your being autistic? Why or why not?

877.

What support inequities have you personally observed?

878.

After watching the video (https://www.youtube.com/watch?v=0rnRxb2NbeI)[43] what is your opinion on the concept of pairing? Do you consider it manipulative, helpful, both, or neither? Why?

879.

When using pairing techniques, does the autistic person retain any personal agency? Why or why not?

880.

In ABA practice, pairing may be used to build the relationship between the practitioner and their client. In this context, do you consider pairing to be manipulative, helpful, both, or neither? Why or why not?

---

[43] Modern Day ABA. (2022). *Building rapport with your learner (pairing)*.

881.

If current ABA practices are as kinder and client-centered as practitioners and supporters claim, differing from past methods, would you support ABA? Why or why not?

882.

To what extent do you agree that an autistic person who needs a lot of support should be treated with the same dignity and respect as someone who has no support needs?

883.

Do you believe that empathy from others is a necessary form of support for autistic people? Why or why not?

884.

If empathy is a support need, who should provide the support? Why?

885.

Is it possible for behavior modification methods to teach people to be empathetic? Why or why not?

886.

How might cultural responsiveness and behaviorism-based interventions be at odds?

887.

Is it possible to be culturally responsive while providing behaviorism-based supports? Why or why not?

888.

If ABA practices were suddenly banned, but all other non-behaviorism based supports for autistic people remained available, who would be the *most* negatively impacted?

- Autistic children
- Parents of autistic children
- ABA providers/practitioners

Why did you select your response?

889.

Would there be any positive outcomes from banning ABA? If so, what would they be and why?

890.

What would be some long-term effects of banning ABA for autistic kids, parents of autistic kids, and those who use ABA services? Why?

891.

Does being "culturally responsive" change anything about the core beliefs and practices of applied behavior analysis? Why or why not?

892.

How would promoting culturally responsive ABA services influence your perception of the ABA industry's efforts to integrate autistic perspectives? Why do you feel this way?

893.

If conditions such as anxiety, epilepsy, depression, and gastrointestinal issues are considered "co-occurring conditions" for autistic people, are they also considered co-occurring conditions for neuromajority people? Why or why not?

894.

What assumptions do we make when we view autism as a "condition" associated with "commonly *co-occurring conditions*"?

895.

If anxiety, epilepsy, etc. are co-occurring conditions, does that mean that autism is a *co-occurring* condition as well? Why or why not?

896.

If autism is considered a co-occurring condition, would being neurotypical also be categorized as a co-occurring condition if the neurotypical person has conditions like anxiety, epilepsy, etc.? Why or why not?

897.

To what extent do you agree or disagree with the statement, "Humans must prove their worthiness to receive support before others are obligated to provide it"?

898.

To what extent do you agree or disagree with the statement, "There is only a certain amount of support humans are willing to provide another before the person needing support becomes a burden"?

899.
To what extent do you agree or disagree with the statement, "All humans rely on other humans for some sort of support"?

900.
If you could write a federal law concerning autism support issues, what specific issues would it target? Why?

901.
Do you feel that capitalists exploit autistics by capitalizing on or contributing to fear mongering around autism? Why or why not?

902.
When you see a fundraising event hosted by an autism organization, how do you feel when you see that same organization supports behaviorism-based support for autistic people? Why?

903.
Are there any autism-related organizations that you like that do *not* endorse behaviorism-based supports? If yes, which ones, and why?

904.
Which autism-related organization(s) do you like that do support behaviorism-based supports? Why do you like them?

905.
Which books on parenting autistic children would you recommend? Why would you recommend them?

906.
Generally speaking, do you view supports for autistic people primarily as:
- Efforts to fix their deficits
- Changes to improve their lives, making it better, easier, or more similar to those who don't struggle

907.
In the autistic context, we hear a lot about treating symptoms and supporting autistic people. Are treating symptoms and supporting autistic people the same thing?

908.
If treating symptoms and supporting autistic people are different, what makes them different?

909.
If treating symptoms and supporting autistic people are viewed as the same, why might an autistic person take offense to the idea of one but not the other?

910.
Should there be limitations on who can provide treatments for "autism symptoms"? Why or why not?

911.
Should there be limitations on who can provide support for autistic people? Why or why not?

912.
How do you define "problematic" and "socially significant" behaviors?

913.
Are there any "problematic" or "socially significant" behaviors that can *only* be "treated" with applied behavior analysis (ABA)? Why or why not?

914.
What assumptions exist about "problematic" and "socially significant" behaviors?

915.
Why do some people believe that observable behaviors should be the target of "treatment" in autistic people?

916.
Does changing behaviors necessarily imply that the person whose behavior has changed also understands those changes? Why or why not?

917.
As humans, do we have any legal, ethical, or moral responsibilities to support disabled individuals? Why or why not?

918.
Would a child identified as autistic between the ages of 2 to 3 have a better adult life, one that is happier and more successful, if they receive therapy as opposed to only supports? Why or why not?

919.
Does your answer to question 918 change depending on the type of therapy offered to the child? Why or why not?

920.

Regarding question 918, what should therapy address for an autistic child ages two to three?

921.

What does successful therapy for an autistic child look like from the perspective of a parent or guardian?

922.

How should an autistic child feel before, during, and after a therapy session for it to be considered successful from their perspective? Does this change with the child's age?

923.

Would ABA practitioners deliver more effective services if they participated in ABA as clients themselves to develop their behavioral artistry? Why or why not?

924.

If you are an ABA practitioner, how would you respond if you were asked to undergo ABA to further develop your ABA practitioner skills? What influences your response?

925.

Is the idea of an ABA practitioner undergoing ABA themselves a ludicrous idea? Why or why not?

926.

If you support ABA, do you ever feel angry when an autistic person advocates against ABA? Why or why not?

Autism, Support, and Services 181

927.

If you do feel angry when an autistic person advocates against ABA, what assumptions do you make about the person?

928.

If you do feel angry when an autistic person advocates against ABA, how would you respond to that person, if you respond at all?

929.

If you do feel angry when an autistic person advocates against ABA, do you research their claims? Why or why not?

930.

If you believe ABA is a positive, beneficial approach to supporting autistic people, why do you think some people completely oppose ABA?

931.

If you believe ABA is a positive, beneficial approach to supporting autistic people, what assumptions do you hold about those who oppose ABA? Why?

932.

If you believe ABA is a positive, beneficial approach to supporting autistic people, what assumptions do you hold about those who support ABA? Why?

933.

What assumptions do you hold about any positive impacts of ABA?

934.

What assumptions do you hold about any negative impacts of ABA?

935.
Is it possible to quantify the support needed by an autistic person, regardless of age? Consider factors such as amount, frequency, and duration of support. Why or why not?

936.
If support needs for autistic people cannot be quantified in a measurable way, how can we assess whether the support being provided is sufficient?

937.
Is the quantity of support needed by autistic people related to the type of support in any way? Why or why not?

938.
Is the quantity of support for autistic people even a relevant consideration? Why or why not?

939.
If you're autistic, do you know how many things for which you need support?

940.
Do autistic adults require more, less, or the same amount of support as autistic children? Why or why not?

941.
When a child is identified as autistic, there is often a focus on providing "treatment" to help them in some way. What might the outcomes be if, instead, the treatment and support were directed toward the parents or caregivers to help them better understand and support the child?

942.
What would the treatment for parents and caregivers, as described in question 941, involve? Why would these methods be used?

943.
How would you feel if the strategy described in question 941 became the standard treatment approach for autism?

944.
What would be the long-term impacts if the approach described in question 941 was used instead of focusing treatment on the autistic child?

945.
Should those who teach adults, such as in higher education or workplace learning, make specific adjustments in their teaching or classroom practices to foster a welcoming learning environment for the autistic adult learners? Why or why not?

946.
What are some specific adjustments a person who teaches adults can make to their teaching or classroom practices to create a more welcoming learning environment for autistic adult learners?

947.
Where does a person learn about the types of adjustments that can be made to create a more welcoming learning environment for adult autistic learners?

948.
If you believe that adjustments are not necessary for adult learners, why do you believe this?

949.

If you teach adults, what memorable experiences have you had teaching autistic adults? Why were they memorable?

950.

If tomorrow we wake up and 99.5% of all parents and caregivers of autistic people reject applied behavior analysis (ABA) as an acceptable support measure for their autistic loved ones, what would happen to the ABA industry? Why?

951.

What assumptions do you have about ABA services?

952.

If ABA services were suddenly rejected, what other services would have to change to deal with this sudden shift in support service demand? Why?

953.

If ABA services were suddenly rejected, what laws and regulations would have to change to deal with this sudden shift in support service demand? Why?

954.

If ABA services were suddenly rejected, how would medical providers have to change to deal with this sudden shift in support service demand? Why?

955.

If ABA services were suddenly rejected, how would schools, universities, and certification programs that offer ABA-related programs and continuing education need to adapt to this sudden shift in support service demand? Why?

956.
If the scenario described in question 955 were to occur, how might the small percentage of parents and caregivers who still support or demand ABA services need to adapt to the sudden shift in support service availability? Why?

957.
According to the Oxford Dictionary, behaviorism is the theory that human and animal behavior can be explained in terms of conditioning, without appeal to thoughts or feelings, and psychological disorders are best treated by altering behavior patterns.

The Oxford Dictionary also defines "compassionate" as feeling or showing sympathy and concern for others, and "kind" as having or showing a friendly, generous, and considerate nature.

Given these definitions, is ABA inherently compassionate and/or kind? Why or why not?

958.
Can ABA be made to be kind and compassionate if it is rooted in behaviorism? Why or why not?

959.
Why might someone decide behaviorism is the best option for teaching autistic people?

960.
Is there a relationship between ABA and capitalism? If so, what is the relationship?

961.

If there is a relationship between ABA and capitalism, is this something that concerns you? What is that concern? Why is it concerning?

962.

If there is a relationship between ABA and capitalism, does the relationship need to be altered? If so, why and how?

963.

If there is a relationship between ABA and capitalism, who benefits from that relationship? Why and how?

964.

Are there other effective methods besides ABA for teaching autistic people how to do things, or is ABA considered the only capable method? Why or why not?

965.

If you believe that ABA is the only effective method to teach autistic people how to do things, which other approaches have you considered or explored?

966.

If you believe that ABA is the only effective method for teaching autistic people because it's "evidence-based," what would your thoughts be upon discovering that other methods also have evidence supporting their effectiveness?

967.

If you believe that ABA is the only way to teach autistic people how to do things, what would persuade you to consider alternatives?

968.

If you believe that ABA is the only effective way to teach autistic people how to do things, what sources lead you to this conclusion?

969.

Is autism commoditized? Why or why not? What is an example to illustrate your perspective?

970.

What is your reaction to Anne McGuire's quote[44] below?

"The notion of spectrum offers a hopeful (which, from the vantage point of capitalism, most often means lucrative) narrative of the possibility for an incremental of normative life."

971.

Are there any "treatments" or "therapies" currently being imposed on autistic people that regard them as not being sentient? If so, what are they?

972.

How might certain treatments or therapies regard autistic people as not being sentient?

973.

If computers were/could be sentient, what applications might they have in identifying support services for autistic people?

---

[44] McGuire, A. (2016). War on autism: on the cultural logic of normative violence. University of Michigan Press.

974.

What would be the advantages and disadvantages of sentient artificial intelligence (AI)[45] assessing and supporting autistic/suspected autistic people?

975.

If you are an ABA practitioner, what emotions do you feel when you hear that some people want ABA to be banned? Why?

976.

If you are an ABA practitioner, does hearing that some people want ABA to be banned make you critically evaluate the ABA field? Why or why not?

977.

If you are an ABA practitioner, and you feel that ABA should *not* be banned, why do you feel that way?

978.

If you are or were an ABA practitioner and you feel that ABA should be banned, why do you feel that way?

979.

If you are an ABA practitioner, what assumptions do you hold about the reasons why some people want to ban ABA?

980.

If you support ABA, are you able to understand the perspectives of those who would like to ban ABA?

---

[45] Artificial intelligence is intelligence — perceiving, synthesizing, and inferring information — demonstrated by machines, as opposed to intelligence displayed by animals and humans.

981.

If you support ABA, what do you want those who want to ban ABA to know? Why do you want them to know this?

982.

What role do physicians play in the continuance of ABA?

983.

If most applied behavior analysts primarily work with autistic clients, should ABA practitioner certification exams include questions about autism and autistic behaviors? Why or why not?

984.

Regardless of one's stance on ABA, is it possible to find common ground and have a fruitful dialogue about autistics' concerns? Why or why not?

985.

Is there value in having dialogue to find common ground between those who support and those who oppose ABA? Why or why not?

986.

If ABA is truly about improving communication and interactions, both of which are two-way processes, shouldn't those who enroll their loved ones in ABA also undergo it themselves? Why or why not?

987.

Which plays the bigger role in requiring more intensive supports: being autistic itself or co-occurring conditions? Why?

988.

For those who were ABA practitioners and have left the field completely, what was the driving force for leaving?

989.

If you were an ABA practitioner and left the field, what specific moment or experience made you decide to leave?

990.

If you were an ABA practitioner and left the field, is there anything you wish you had done differently that is not related to client interactions, but to the field itself?

991.

If you were an ABA practitioner and left the field, what advice would you give other ABA practitioners? Why?

992.

If you were an ABA practitioner and left the field, what are one to three paradigm changes you believe should take place? Why?

993.

If you were an ABA practitioner and left the field, what direction has your professional journey taken since leaving ABA?

994.

Do you feel leaving the ABA field after attaining a doctorate-level education might be viewed as a waste of educational achievement? Why or why not?

995.
If you were an ABA practitioner and left the field, would you ever return to being an ABA practitioner? Why or why not?

996.
Why is there a continued push for ABA despite significant opposition?

997.
If research demonstrates a link between ABA and psychological trauma, do behavior analysts have an obligation to educate clients about this? Why or why not?

998.
Do behavior analysts have an obligation to stop services if their client is being traumatized by those same services? Why or why not?

999.
For those who support using ABA to help autistic people (however you define "help"), which of these two reinforcement approaches is more ethical:

- Positive reinforcement: Adding a pleasant stimulus in response to a desired behavior.
- Negative reinforcement: Rewarding a desired behavior by removing an unpleasant stimulus.

1,000.
If you said only one reinforcement method noted in question 999 is ethical, why is the other not ethical?

1,001.

If you said neither reinforcement methods noted in question 999 are ethical, why?

1,002.

What assumptions do you have about using reinforcers to change behavior?

1,003.

Where is the dividing line between reinforcing desired behaviors and coercing people to behave in ways that are unnatural for them?

1,004.

What are some examples of acceptable positive reinforcers?

1,005.

What are some examples of unacceptable positive reinforcers?

1,006.

What are some examples of acceptable negative reinforcers?

1,007.

What are some examples of unacceptable negative reinforcers?

1,008.

Do you think focusing on changing behavior (e.g., through education or behavioral health treatment) is the best way to improve people's lives? Why or why not?

1,009.

If not behavior, what other focus should we have when it comes to improving people's lives? Why?

1,010.

Does a change in outward behavior always indicate a change in thinking or cognition about that behavior? Why or why not?

1,011.

If you've participated in ABA and also occupational therapy, speech therapy, or similar, was your experience with ABA the same or different than with the others?

1,012.

If you've participated in both ABA and occupational therapy, how did you feel after each type of session?

1,013.

Does ABA *primarily* aim to help people:
- Do something right
- Do the right thing
- Decide what is right[46]

1,014.

What if behavior modification approaches to "treating" autism are eventually seen as just another failed medical intervention from the past?

1,015.

Is it possible that the current thinking held by many in behavior modification as the "gold standard" for helping autistic people is incorrect? Why or why not?

---

[46] These three response options were derived from the Triple-Loop learning model. In single-loop learning, the focus is on the actions—questioning whether or not we are doing things the right way. In double-loop learning, the focus is on our assumptions—questioning whether or not we are doing the right things. In triple-loop learning, the focus is on the context—questioning how we decide what is right.

1,016.

Is there an ethical obligation to stop ABA practices based on the Hippocratic Oath?[47]

1,017.

Many autistic people have voiced concerns about behavior modification for some time. Should their perspectives be considered in deciding what's best for autistic people? Why or why not?

1,018.

Are the focus of "treatments" on autism itself, or is it on something else, such as a co-occurring condition? Why or why not?

1,019.

If you believe behavior modification is the best approach to helping autistic people, are there situations where you'd say it is *not* the best approach for an autistic person? Why?

1,020.

Is it possible that behavior modification, dubbed the "gold standard" in helping autistic people, is actually harmful? Why or why not?

1,021.

If you were an ABA practitioner and left the field, what should be included in ABA education programs that are not currently included? Why?

---

[47] The Hippocratic Oath, a guiding ethical code for physicians, emphasizes the principle of "first, do no harm," which mandates that medical professionals prioritize the well-being of patients by avoiding actions that could cause unnecessary harm or suffering.

1,022.

If you were an ABA practitioner and left the field, what do you wish you knew about ABA before you entered the field? Why?

1,023.

If you were an ABA practitioner and left the field, what benefits did you see with ABA for autistic clients? For parents/family? For the general public?

1,024.

If an autistic adult wanted to pursue ABA treatment to "treat their autism" and stop "acting awkward" in public, would that be an acceptable choice? Why or why not?

1,025.

Should consent be required of anyone receiving ABA, regardless of age? Why or why not?

1,026.

Assuming there were no legal age restrictions, what is the youngest age at which someone should be able to consent to or refuse ABA? Why?

1,027.

What factors should be considered when asking for consent to provide ABA? Why?

1,028.

What factors should be considered when consenting to ABA? Why?

1,029.

What things do you consider when deciding whether to financially support an autism organization? Why?

1,030.

What is the single most important factor to you when deciding to financially support an autism organization? Why?

1,031.

Is there an autism organization you supported in the past but no longer do? What caused you to withdraw your support?

1,032.

Are there any factors that are absolutely non-negotiable for you when it comes to supporting an autism organization? Why?

1,033.

Would you provide financial support to an organization without publicly endorsing them or encouraging others to support? Why or why not?

1,034.

Are you able to state the *specific* support needs someone may have and when they might need them if that person is labeled, "autistic, level one"? Why or why not?

1,035.

If you are an ABA practitioner, do you consider cognition and cognitive processes to be behaviors? Why or why not?

1,036.

Does behavior modification change:

- The way a person thinks?

- A person's sensory perception?

- A person's emotions?

Why or why not?

1,037.

If behavior modification changes any of the things noted in question 1,036, how do you know?

1,038.

If you are an ABA practitioner, do you rely only on observable behaviors to make therapeutic decisions? If not, what else do you use?

1,039.

Is there a difference between learned behaviors and conditioned behaviors? If so, what?

1,040.

If learned behaviors and conditioned behaviors are different, which one is more advantageous? Why?

1,041.

How are learned behaviors and conditioned behaviors similar?

1,042.

When it comes to modifying behaviors, are all approaches the same if they produce the same outcome—a specific desired behavior? Why or why not?

1,043.

If a behavior causes absolutely no harm to the person performing the behavior or to anyone else, but it isn't viewed as a social norm, should it be modified? Why or why not?

1,044.

If the behavior noted in question 1,043 is acceptable in some micro-groups, but not in others, should it be modified? Why or why not?

1,045.

Is it important to have autistic people in top leadership positions in autism organizations? Why or why not?

1,046.

How does the mission of an autism organization influence your decision to provide financial support?

1,047.

Do the programs supported or offered by autism organizations influence your decision to provide financial support? Why or why not?

1,048.

If an autism organization helps to fund research you find objectionable, would you still donate to them? Why or why not?

1,049.

If a friend of yours supports an autism organization you oppose, would you talk with them to understand why they support that organization? Why?

1,050.

Are there any "losses," "injuries," "hazards," "perils," or "dangers" a person is at risk of by merely being autistic? If so, what and by whom?

1,051.

If autism is a naturally occurring neurology, then is there truly any "risk" involved? Why or why not?

1,052.

If you used to work in a role supporting or providing ABA to autistic children, but no longer do, what prompted you to stop?

Chapter 6 Wrap-Up

After reading through the questions in this chapter, pause for a moment to consider the insights you've gained.

1. Which questions made you really think about how autistic people are supported currently? Why? Note the question number as part of your response.

2. How might you change how you would support autistic people in your life?

3. If you had the opportunity to speak to an elected representative about autism support, what would you say to them in light of the questions posed in this chapter?

4. Draft an email to one of your elected officials about autism support. Send it.

Chapter 7
Autism Advocacy

"To be an activist is to speak. To be an advocate is to listen. Society can't move forward without both."

~ Eva Marie Lewis

Three years ago, I would never have guessed I would be an autistic advocate, much less writing a book about autism advocacy. Now, there are countless people who read my work, engage with me about issues affecting the autistic community, and even some who have made profound changes in their lives as a result of something I posted online. When I think about it, I can feel overwhelmed by the awesome responsibility that comes with advocacy, but I also feel encouraged by the dialogue that results from my posts. It truly is a benefit to advocate for myself and for the community.

From my young advocate perspective, I see the role of advocates in the autistic community as being a voice to promote understanding of the autistic experience and help to change the current system that marginalizes autistic people. They work to educate autistics, parents, and professionals alike about the experiences autistic people have in a world not necessarily built for them. They work to dismantle stereotypes and stigmas that burden autistic people. They also address inequalities in the areas of education, healthcare, employment, and other basic human rights.

Advocates in the autistic community come in a variety of forms, each with a somewhat different purpose in their advocacy work. The primary advocates include, but are not limited to:

- Non-autistic parents of autistic children, who provide insights into a different, but challenging nonetheless, experience adjacent to the autistic person themselves. Often, non-autistic parents focus on advocating for their children and ensuring that they receive appropriate support and accommodations, which may or may not align with what autistic people support. They may also advocate for increased research and funding for autism-related services, as well as for greater understanding and acceptance of autism in society.
- Healthcare and support providers, who are often not autistic themselves, work to promote what they believe to be the best possible care for autistic people. Sometimes this involves greater training for providers to improve their diagnostic abilities, improved treatments, and better access to care and support services. These advocates are also frequently involved with research, which like the care they provide is almost always steeped in the medical model of disability.
- Educators, who teach healthcare and support providers also advocate for autistic people. Their focus is often on the next generation of professionals to be more aware of autism and autism treatments, which is also almost always steeped in the medical model of disability. They advocate for curriculum changes and other measures that increase autism awareness and encourage the development of more autism-friendly policies and practices in the healthcare system.
- Actually autistic advocates, who provide a first-person account of the challenges autistic people face, especially in areas of accessibility, proper supports, human rights, and social justice issues. They aim to build acceptance of autism as a valid way of being and to appreciate neurodiversity.

Autistic advocates may also focus on changing the way that society approaches and accommodates autism.

Unfortunately, the most important advocate, those that are actually autistic, are more likely to be subjugated and dismissed. Actually autistic advocates, whether as a self-advocate or advocate at large, autistic voices are all too often spoken over by others who most likely are not autistic. Their experiences tend to not be taken seriously, especially when it comes to the trauma[48] caused by a cure culture. Despite these advocacy challenges, there is a brighter future – one where the autistic voices continue to gain a strong foothold in the autism narrative and one that has already affected a change in the messaging ABA practitioners use to promote their services.

In this chapter, questions focus on many perspectives of advocacy work and the advocates themselves. You'll explore the intersection of person, support, and outcomes while challenging some strongly-held perspectives that the autism industrial complex (AIC)[49] set into motion in the 1980's and 1990's. Be prepared to reset your expectations for autism advocacy.

---

[48] For more on this assertion, see: Kupferstein, H. (2018). Evidence of increased PSTD symptoms in autistics exposed to applied behavior analysis. *Advances in Autism, 4*(1), 19-29. doi: 10.1108/AIA-08-2017-0016.

[49] The autism industrial complex (AIC) is the term given to the complex network of culture, narrative, commodification, and capitalization of autism and autism interventions in the book, *The Autism Industrial Complex: How Branding, Marketing, And Capital Investment Turned Autism Into Big Business"* by Alicia A. Broderick. This is a **highly** recommended reading.

1,053.

Would it be appropriate to refer to non-autistic (neuromajority) people as being on a spectrum of their own? Why or why not?

1,054.

If you're not autistic (neuromajority), how would you feel being referred to as "on the spectrum"? Would it be offensive? Why or why not?

1,055.

Can autistic and non-autistic people come together to re-imagine the expectations of human interaction? Why or why not?

1,056

If you think autistic and non-autistic people can come together to re-imagine the expectations of human interaction, what do you think would change? Why?

1,057.

If you don't think autistic and non-autistic people can come together to re-imagine the expectations of human interaction, what do you believe stops us?

1,058.

Assuming that autistic people do have communication difficulties, would it be accurate or fair to say that non-autistic people also have communication difficulties? Why or why not?

1,059.

What unchallenged assumptions about autism persist, including misconceptions that many believe to be true? Why do these assumptions remain unchallenged?

1,060.
What obstacles exist that prevent people from challenging conventional wisdom about autism? Why?

1,061.
Are there certain understandings about autistic people and autism that should not be critically examined or challenged? Why or why not?

1,062.
What are the dangers of not challenging assumptions about autistic people and autism? Why?

1,063.
How frequently do you question whether or not your advocacy efforts are worth the emotional labor you invest? Why?

1,064.
What originally motivated you to become an autistic advocate?

1,065.
What continues to motivate you to be or become an autistic advocate?

1,066.
How do you deal with those who try to squash your advocacy efforts?

1,067.
What are the most common things people challenge in your advocacy efforts?

1,068.

What do you believe is the most fundamental thing that unites autistic advocates? Why?

1,069.

What do you think would happen if you suddenly stopped advocating for autistic people and the autistic community? What would happen if all advocates for autistics and the autistic community suddenly stopped?

1,070.

What would happen if all advocates for autistics and the autistic community suddenly stopped?

1,071.

What can you personally do today to positively impact how autistic people feel?

1,072.

If listening to others' perspectives about autism, even those whose perspectives are polar opposite of yours, causes you to critically reflect and you revise your own perspective as a result, is this a good, bad, or neutral thing? Why?

1,073.

Is it good, bad, or neutral to listen to others' perspectives about autism, critically reflect, and revise your own perspective? Why?

1,074.

What topics regarding autism, especially in the contexts of the workplace, learning, and advocacy, are you interested in exploring? Why?

1,075.

If you're a psychology or ABA student, how do you feel about the stances many in the autistic community have on issues that contradict what you are taught in your courses?

1,076.

If you're a psychology or ABA student, are you open to engaging in dialogue with autistic people to understand their experiences beyond a medical or deficit perspective? Why or why not?

1,077.

What do you want autistic advocates to keep doing? Why?

1,078.

What do you want advocates to do more of? Why?

1,079.

What do you want autistic advocates to do less of? Why?

1,080.

What do you want autistic advocates to start doing? Why?

1,081.

What do you want autistic advocates to stop doing? Why?

1,082.

What might happen if autism advocacy efforts targeted universities teaching psychology, especially with psychologists and neuroscientists who identify as neurodivergent leading the way? Why?

1,083.

Would the efforts described in question 1,082 have a positive or negative effect on individual autistic people? Why?

1,084.

Could the efforts described in question 1,082 change policy decisions at federal, state, and local levels? Why or why not?

1,085.

How could the efforts described in question 1,082 change certifying organizations and licensing boards for psychology and related fields? Why?

1,086.

What should be the goal of autism advocacy? Why?

1,087.

Do you differentiate between autistic advocates who advocate for all autistic people and those who advocate for only some autistic people? If so, how?

1,088.

Could a non-autistic person be conditioned to stim when stressed, assuming they don't already stim? Would it be ethical? Why or why not?

1,089.

Have you encountered an autistic advocate who advocates for only certain, but not all, autistic people? Describe your interaction.

1,090.
Why do you think some autistic advocates only advocate for certain autistic people, but not all?

1,091.
Should autistic advocates always advocate for all autistic people? Why or why not?

1,092.
Are autistic advocates who advocate for only certain autistic people harmful or helpful to the autistic community? Why?

1,093.
When people refer to the neurodiversity movement as a social justice or civil rights movement, do you think this applies to all autistic people, regardless of support needs, or only to certain autistic people? Why or why not?

1,094.
If the neurodiversity movement is a social justice and/or civil rights movement for *all* autistic people, what are some reasons someone might argue it isn't?

1,095.
If the neurodiversity movement is seen as a social justice and/or civil rights movement for only certain autistic people, what are some reasons others might argue it benefits all autistic people?

1,096.
What criticisms might you have about the neurodiversity movement?

1,097.

What are some benefits of the neurodiversity movement?

1,098.

Do you feel the neurodiversity movement romanticizes autism? Why or why not?

1,099.

Have you personally witnessed or experienced any harm as a result of the neurodiversity movement? If so, what happened? Has it continued to affect you over time?

1,100.

What primary role does an autistic advocate serve?

1,101.

What will it take to convince the world that *all* autistic people are more than a collection of their behaviors?

1,102.

If we woke up tomorrow and autism were defined not by behavior deficits (e.g., communication, socialization, etc.), but as a cognitive difference in thinking (e.g., perception, problem-solving, etc.) without observable behavior differences, how would that change the way we interact with autistic people? Why?

1,103.

If the change described in question 1,102 were to happen, how would that impact the ways we provide care and support for any challenges autistic people experience?

1,104.

If the change described in question 1,102 were to happen, how might this benefit and/or harm autistic people? Why?

1,105.

If the change described in question 1,102 were to happen, would there still be a worry that without help, an autistic child might not be successful or independent later in life? Why or why not?

1,106.

A hypothetical situation to consider:

You are a parent of a child who was diagnosed with what you call "moderate autism." She's able to do many self-care things on her own, but still needs help, has some difficulty speaking, and doesn't have many friends. Over the past three years, she's been in ABA, loves her therapist, and according to the therapist's data and your own observations, she has "improved significantly."

Recently, you've been looking to move and the most perfect and incredible living situation you could ever contemplate presented itself. It's in a completely different location with every imaginable opportunity available. What's more, money is not an issue. You gave the situation all due diligence possible and decided to move.

Once in your new living situation, you make some calls to set up therapy appointments for your child. You learn that not only are there no ABA providers, ABA of any form has been completely banned in the community. Reluctantly, you agree to go to a different sort of therapist and set up the earliest appointment, which is in three weeks.

Within a couple weeks of her beginning therapy, you begin to realize that your daughter's teachers don't complain about her having any "bad behaviors." In fact, your daughter tells you about how many new friends she has and was invited to a birthday party.

You also notice a stark difference in how your new friends and neighbors interact with your daughter. Even in public, there is a palpable difference in how the environment feels (less noise, fewer distractions, etc.) and how strangers react when your daughter does things that you believed were "socially inappropriate." There seems to be a completely different culture in this community regarding autism—a very positive, affirming culture.

At home, your daughter seems to be happier and is enjoying school. While she isn't learning the same things at the same time as her classmates, she is learning and her teachers seem to know how to support her learning needs. Even though she still has challenges speaking, she seems to have experienced an awakening of sorts and appears to be flourishing now.

Does this scenario seem far-fetched to you? Why or why not?

1,107.
If this scenario in question 1,106 seems far-fetched to you, which part(s) are not realistic? Why?

1,108.
If this were you in the scenario described in question 1,106, would you continue with the therapy? Why or why not?

1,109.
Imagine we wake up to a world where more than 80% of the population is identified as autistic. What would happen to the ABA industry? Why?

1,110.
If we woke up to a world where more than 80% of the population is identified as autistic, would there be a need to change the non-autistic population's behavior to something that was "socially appropriate" using behavior modification methods? Why or why not?

1,111.
Would stimming in autistic people be more prevalent, less prevalent, or equally prevalent if they were the majority of the population? Why or why not?

1,112.
How would the Diagnostic and Statistical Manual of Mental Disorders (DSM) differ if autistic people were the largest majority? Why?

1,113.
Why are people purposefully marginalizing autistic people? Who benefits from this power dynamic?

1,114.
Could cultural changes regarding autism have a dramatically positive impact on the lives of autistic people? Why or why not?

1,115.
Whose interests are served by framing autism in a way that maintains a power dynamic favoring the neuromajority? Why?

1,116.

What assumptions do we have regarding the power dynamics between autistic people and non-autistic people? What perpetuates these assumptions?

1,117.

What prevents us from challenging assumptions about autistic people and autism to create a new reality that is beneficial to *all*? Why?

1,118.

If every possible support were available to anyone in need, without cost or restriction, would there still be a reason to assess and classify any neurodivergency? Why or why not?

1,119.

In a world where supports would be provided without restriction, what purpose would identifying specific neurodivergences serve?

1,120.

In a world where supports would be provided without restriction, who would ultimately benefit from identifying specific neurodivergences? Why would they benefit?

1,121.

In a world where supports would be provided without restriction, would there be harm caused by identifying specific neurodivergences? If so, who would be harmed and in what ways? Why?

1,122.

Does the idea of reconceptualizing and redefining autism excite you? Why or why not?

1,123.

Would your answer to question 1,122 be the same if you considered it from the perspective of an autistic person (if you're not autistic) or a non-autistic person (if you are autistic)? Why or why not?

1,124.

What would be possible benefits of reconceptualizing and redefining autism?

1,125.

What would be some of the downsides of reconceptualizing and redefining autism? Why?

1,126.

How might reconceptualizing and redefining autism impact societal perceptions and acceptance of autistic people?

1,127.

If reconceptualizing and redefining autism resulted in 100% coverage for 100% of support needs for *all* autistic people, regardless of how many, how frequently, or how intensive the supports were, etc., would you endorse such an endeavor? Why or why not?

1,128.

If reconceptualizing and redefining autism resulted in double the number of people identified as autistic, would you endorse such an endeavor? What if the number tripled? What if the number quadrupled? Why or why not?

1,129.

Does the idea of reconceptualizing and redefining autism scare you? Why or why not?

1,130.

Would it be accurate to say that ~80% of what is "understood" about autism is a result of ~20% of the autistic population? Why or why not?

1,131.

Would it be accurate to say that ~80% of available supports for autistic people is marketed to ~20% of the autistic population? Why or why not?

1,132.

Would it be accurate to say that only ~20% of the autistic population have gainful employment? Why or why not?

1,133.

At this point in the neurodiversity movement, should all neurodivergences be reconceptualized? Why or why not?

1,134.

How can our neurology be perceived as one thing in the context of autism, but be seen as an environment for conditions like depression in the neurotypical context? Why do you think this difference in perspectives exists?

1,135.

If autism is conceptualized as a neurotype, how can it "co-occur" with conditions like depression or anxiety, which are not considered neurotypes? Alternatively, could depression and anxiety be viewed as neurotypes and, thus, an environment in which autism occurs? Why or why not?

1,136.

Does autism actually *co-occur* with other things (such as depression, anxiety, etc.)? Why or why not?

1,137.

Would anything change about how autistic people are perceived if "condition" was not included in any descriptive language regarding autism? Why or why not?

1,138.

What is the source of motivation for providing supports for autistic people, however you define "supports"? Does it differ based on which group is providing the support?

1,139.

According to Singer[50], while there is no official definition or spokesperson for the [neurodiversity] movement, its consensual aims can be discerned. They are to:
- Shift mainstream perceptions of marginalized NeuroMinorities.
- Replace negative, deficit-based stereotypes of NeuroMinorities with a more balanced valuation of their gifts and needs.
- Find valued roles for neurologically marginalized people.
- Show that all society benefits from the incorporation of NeuroMinorities.

---

[50] Singer, J. (n.d.). *Reflections on neurodiversity*. https://lnkd.in/gSh4h3-Q

With the above in mind, can someone fully support neurodiversity movement aims listed above while also advocating for ABA?

1,140.
If you do *not* believe support for the neurodiversity movement and ABA can happen together, why do you think so?

1,141.
If you believe support for the neurodiversity movement and ABA can happen together, why do you think so?

1,142.
What would be the result if, instead of supporting autistic people to be independent, we simply supported their needs? Why?

1,143.
Is it possible that autistic children who cannot do something for themselves now will be able to do it in the future if we do it for them in the interim? Why or why not?

1,144.
If an autistic person can never do something for themselves, is that a bad thing? Why or why not?

1,145.
Is it more important to provide support to someone, even if it's inconvenient, than to let them live without that support? Why or why not?

1,146.

Is independent living the true goal of providing supports? Why or why not?

1,147.

Is independent living an altruistic goal? Why or why not?

1,148.

If independent living is the true goal of providing supports, why is that the case?

1,149.

How can we unite to support the needs of autistic people by reducing or eliminating environmental, societal, and other barriers, rather than focusing on fixing perceived autistic deficits?

1,150.

How can we make it perfectly okay to be autistic in all situations, environments, and contexts?

1,151.

What would be different about how we view autism if Socrates, John Locke[51], or Confucious[52] influenced the study of what we now know as autism? Why?

1,152.

Would autism be conceptualized completely differently had it came to the forefront at a different historical time? Why or why not?

---

[51] John Locke was an English philosopher and physician, who was widely regarded as one of the most influential of Enlightenment thinkers and commonly known as the "father of liberalism."
[52] Confucius was a Chinese philosopher who taught ethics, personal morality, and proper governance. He emphasized the importance of virtue, education, and leading by moral example, advocating for a harmonious society based on benevolence, righteousness, and proper conduct.

1,153.

Imagine if autism's "coming of age" occurred during a different time period—one that was not dominated by behaviorism? How would the autism construct look today if it were more heavily influenced by philosophical thoughts such as Freudianism[53], Jungianism[54], humanism[55], cognitivism[56], or something else?

1,154.

Are we beholden to view autism through a behavioristic lens? Why or why not?

1,155.

How can an autistic autism advocate with few support needs effectively advocate for themselves and for other autistic individuals who have more significant support needs?

1,156.

To what degree is it acceptable to challenge the neuromajority's narrative about autism? Why?

---

[53] Freudianism suggests that human behavior is influenced by unconscious memories, thoughts, and urges.

[54] Jungianism is an in-depth, analytical form of talk therapy designed to bring together the conscious and unconscious parts of the mind to help a person feel balanced and whole.

[55] Humanism is a system of thought attaching prime importance to human rather than divine or supernatural matters. Humanist beliefs stress the potential value and goodness of human beings, emphasize common human needs, and seek solely rational ways of solving human problems.

[56] Cognitivism is the study in psychology that focuses on mental processes, including how people perceive, think, remember, learn, solve problems, and direct their attention to one stimulus rather than another.

1,157.
In what ways is it beneficial that people are challenging the neuromajority narratives about autism and autistic people? In what ways might it be problematic?

1,158.
What aspects about challenging the neuromajority narrative do you see as causing a negative reaction from autistic people? From non-autistic people?

1,159.
What aspects about challenging the neuromajority narrative do you see as causing a positive reaction from autistic people? From non-autistic people?

1,160.
What are potential unintentional consequences of challenging the neuromajority narrative about autism that could cause harm to autistic people?

1,161.
What qualifies someone to be a true autism advocate, capable of advocating for all autistic individuals, not just themselves? Why?

1,162.
Is there anything that disqualifies someone from being an autistic advocate? Why or why not?

1,163.
How do you differentiate between an autism advocate and autistic self-advocate? Why?

1,164.

If someone is advocating for a cause, must they present only those perspectives with which the entire community agrees 100%? Why or why not?

1,165.

How much room do advocates have to represent their personal views or views that are not universally shared by the entire community? Why?

1,166.

How do you react when someone advocates for something a large percentage of the autistic community supports, but you personally do not?

1,167.

What happens when we ask questions about multiple perspectives of art from a wide range of artists and non-artists?
- Less understanding of art
- No change in understanding of art
- Greater understanding of art

Why did you select your answer?

1,168.

What would happen if art was only explored from one perspective, and never explored from multiple perspectives? Why?

1,169.

Does asking about multiple perspectives of art help uncover assumptions? If so, how?

1,170.
How can asking questions about art bring about change faster than merely asserting a position on any given issue in art?

1,171.
What happens when we ask questions about multiple perspectives on autism from a wide range of autistic and non-autistic people?
- Less understanding of autism
- No change in understanding of autism
- Greater understanding of autism

Why did you select your answer?

1,172.
What would happen if we don't explore multiple perspectives about autism? Why?

1,173.
Does asking about multiple perspectives of autism help uncover assumptions? If so, how?

1,174.
How can asking questions about autism bring about change faster than merely asserting a position on any given issue?

1,175.
Should people have the right to self-determination? Why or why not?

1,176.
Are there limits to self-determination? If so, what are these limits?

1,177.

Does self-determination differ for adults and children? Why or why not?

1,178.

Should self-determination differ between autistic people and non-autistic people? Why or why not?

1,179.

What are the key factors in deciding who has rights to self-determination and who does not?

1,180.

Has the neurodiversity movement truly been elevated to a social justice movement? Why or why not?

1,181.

If the neurodiversity movement has not been truly elevated to a social justice movement, what will it take to get it to a social justice movement status? Why?

1,182.

Do autistic people need social justice? Why or why not?

1,183.

What have you personally observed that indicates whether an autistic social justice movement is or is not taking place?

1,184.

Is social justice for autistic and other neurodivergent people a good or bad thing? Why?

1,185.
What can you personally contribute to the neurodiversity movement that would help bring about a more egalitarian society for autistic people?

1,186.
Should autistic people bear the burden to change? Why or why not?

1,187.
As a parent, would your level of worry differ if your child were identified as autistic during their youth compared to being identified as autistic in adulthood? What might be the reasons for any differences in your level of fear or concern?

1,188.
Which of these two options would best serve humanity?
- Molding people to "fit in"
- Accepting people's differences

1,189.
What does Autism Acceptance month mean to you?

1,190.
Consider this hypothetical situation: We wake up in a new world. Everything is the same *except* these three things:
- There is *zero* stigma associated with autism or being autistic
- Non-autistic people 100% accept autistic people for who they are, as-is
- Ample supports/adjustments for autistic peoples' needs are readily available and implemented

How would these three things change your life?

1,191.

How different would Autism Acceptance Month look (or would it even exist) if the three things described in question 1,190 happened?

1,192.

If the three things described in 1,190 happened, would the principles and practices of "assume competence"[57] for autistic individuals change? If so, how and why?

1,193.

If the three things described in question 1,190 happened, would the world be a better place for everyone to live? Why or why not?

1,194.

If the three things described in question 1,190 happened, would autism still be included in the DSM or ICD? Why or why not?

1,195.

If the three things described in question 1,190 occurred, would the medical/deficit model still be applied to other disabilities? Why or why not?

1,196.

If the three things described in question 1,190 happened, would ABA services exist? Why or why not?

1,197.

If the three things described in question 1,190 happened, would research still exist to find autism's "cause" or "cures?" Why or why not?

---

[57] "Assumed competence" is the belief that someone can perform a task or has knowledge without requiring explicit proof.

1,198.

If the three things described in question 1,190 happened, would we still use "on the spectrum" when referring to autistic people? Why or why not?

1,199.

If the three things described in question 1,190 happened, would person-first language exist or be used in its current manner? Why or why not?

1,200.

If the three things described in question 1,190 happened, what would autism organizations' mission statements be?

1,201.

Who are some of the most influential autism advocates you know of who are actually autistic and support a neurodiversity-affirming perspective?

1,202.

Thinking about the advocates you highlighted in question 1,201, what key issues do they address in their advocacy work?

1,203.

When engaging in autism advocacy discussions about ABA, some supporters or providers might become defensive and abruptly end the conversation when questioned about their principles and practices. Some consider this response as maladaptive behavior[58].

---

[58] Maladaptive behaviors are actions that prevent people from adapting, adjusting, or participating in different aspects of life. Such actions are intended to help relieve or avoid stress, but they are often disruptive and may contribute to increased distress, discomfort, and anxiety over time.

Based on this description, do you think the ABA supporter/provider is exhibiting maladaptive behavior? Why or why not?

1,204.
If the behavior described in question 1,203 is considered maladaptive, why might an ABA supporter or provider respond in such a way?

1,205.
If the behavior described in question 1,203 is *not* considered maladaptive, what might explain why becoming defensive and abruptly ending a conversation is seen as an appropriate response?

1,206.
How can two people with very different views on ABA engage in a meaningful and respectful conversation about the topic, ensuring that neither side becomes upset or shuts down? What are some ways to help make this happen?

1,207.
If a group consisted mostly of autistic people (say, 80%-90%), would it be acceptable for the autistic members to use rewards and punishments to condition the non-autistic members to conform to group behavior norms? Why or why not?

1,208.
In a community as described in 1,207, are there certain non-autistic behaviors that should remain unconditioned and preserved among the non-autistic people?

1,209.
If we wake up tomorrow and every person on earth has the same neurological design, would the world and humanity be better or worse? Why?

1,210.

If we wake up tomorrow and every person on earth has the same neurological design, how would the world and humanity be better? What did neurodiversity do before to make it worse?

1,211.

If we wake up tomorrow and every person on earth has the same neurological design, how would the world and humanity be worse? What did neurodiversity do before to make it better?

1,212.

Reflecting on your answers to questions 1,2100 and 1,211, what underlying assumptions about neurodiversity do you hold that influenced your responses?

1,213.

If everyone on earth had the same neurological design starting from tomorrow, would the world continue to advance technologically at the same pace as it has up to now? Why or why not?

1,214.

If neurodiversity never existed, would the world still have the same variety in:

- Languages
-Religions
- Political systems
- Economic systems
- Arts
- Educational programs

Why or why not?

1,215.
In general, do autism advocates neglect advocating for those autistics who require significant support for daily living? Why or why not?

1,216.
Do autistic advocates and self-advocates sometimes overlook the needs of the most vulnerable and marginalized members of the autistic community? If so, in what ways does this happen?

1,217.
If you're autistic and have significant support needs, have you ever felt left out by advocates who seemingly focus on those with fewer support needs? What experiences led you to feel this way?

1,218.
What specific actions or statements by autistic advocates would make you feel that they're not advocating for autistic people with significant support needs?

1,219.
What can autistic advocates do to ensure autistic people with significant support needs feel included in their advocacy work?

1,220.
What would advocating for autistic people with significant support needs look like?

1,221.
What negative impacts have you experienced as a result of being excluded from autistic advocacy work?

1,222.

What assumptions do you have about autism advocates with fewer support needs compared to those with higher support needs when it comes to their advocacy messages or approach?

1,223.

What activism[59] efforts are needed to create positive social and political changes to improve the lives of autistic people? Why?

1,224.

As an autistic person, what do you want the world to know about your world perspectives?

1,225.

How do YOU define autism?

1,226.

Imagine a world where the autistic community is viewed as one you most want it to be five years from now.
- What is that new reality like?
- What do you see and hear?
- What do autistic people experience daily?
- How do you feel in this new reality?
- What makes you feel the most alive in this new reality?

---

[59] Activism is vigorous campaigning to bring about political or social change.

Chapter 7 Wrap-Up

After reading this final chapter of questions, take some time to reflect on the experiences and thoughts you've encountered along the way.

1. In what ways have your perspectives of autistic advocates changed (or not changed)?

2. Which questions about autism advocacy made you question the state of autism supports? Why? Note the question number as part of your response.

3. Who is responsible for autism advocacy? Why?

4. If you were to become an advocate for autistic people today, where would you focus your advocacy work? Why?

Chapter 8
All Perspectives Are Valid

"Each person does see the world in a different way. There is not a single, unifying, objective truth. We're all limited by our perspective."

~Siri Hustvedt

Congratulations on reaching the end of the 1,226 reflective questions. This journey through introspection, critical thinking, and emotional exploration has likely stirred many thoughts and feelings within you. As you reflect on the questions you've pondered, consider the diverse perspectives and experiences that have shaped your responses. This process has been designed to challenge your views and expand your understanding of autism, the autistic identity, and the broader autism and autistic communities. With this foundation, we now move into an exploration of these themes through essays that offer further insights and reflections.

My advocacy work often focuses on autistic people's support needs. A relevant topic within this broad area is being a voice for those who have support needs but may not be able to speak for themselves. Within this narrower topic, the types of supports, access to those supports, the means for requesting or demanding those supports, and the actual provision of supports are among the many specific issues I frequently hear and read about, specifically, the challenges autistic people and their loved ones' faces. These narratives are often emotionally charged and rightfully so for many reasons —all of which are valid as they are the lived experiences of those involved.

Frequently, the obstacles autistic people face and the reasons for those challenges are obvious. One example of this is supports needed versus supports offered. An autistic person may need support communicating, but is subjected to conditioning "therapies" to help them speak. In this example, there is a deep divide between those who advocate for and those who advocate against this type of support. On one hand, some will say these "therapies" help while others say they are harmful, each providing their perspectives as to why. For each, *their* perspective on the matter is valid in that it is their lived reality. This is not to say that one side is right and the other is wrong; rather, all perspectives are valid in the eyes of the individual.

All Perspectives are Valid

Every individual has a lifetime of experiences, learnings, and influences that impact how they view the world. These factors inform their perspectives and are continually shaped by their values, beliefs, and assumptions. What one person sees as "wrong" another person may see as "right." But does "right" or "wrong" really exist? What is the "truth?"

Whether there is an absolute truth about anything will always be debated. The presence or absence of truth will not change the conflicts that arise between those who see things differently. Like two people who look at the number "9" drawn on the ground by viewing it from the top of the number or the bottom, the "truth" is based largely in perspective and each perspective is correct. When we face these sorts of perspective differences, things can get tricky, especially when people's well-being is involved, and everyone wants to "do what's best." The most important thing to remember in this situation is that all perspectives are valid, and there is something we can learn from others' perspectives.

Seek to Understand, Then Seek to be Understood

Let's return to the opening example of autistic support in the form of conditioning "therapies." Yes—there are studies that show its harm. Yes—people live with trauma as a result of these "therapies." I don't debate these assertions. In fact, I agree with these assertions and that these supports for autistic people should be eliminated, but this is just *my* perspective. Those who believe these "therapies" are harmful have their reasons and their perspective is 100% correct for them. It is their truth, and it cannot be removed; however, there are others that hold a different perspective. For those who believe these "therapies" are beneficial, they have their reasons and their perspective is 100% correct for them. It is their truth, and it cannot be removed. Trying to land on a universally agreed upon perspective on this subject will most likely never happen and it's futile to aim for such a "truth" that all will accept.

Sharing findings from studies and personal experiences may provide others with insights into one's perspective, but even the most well-reasoned argument is more likely to fail than succeed in changing others' perspectives. The reason is rooted in each individual's worldview, which took a lifetime to acquire. When the subject of any effort to change perspectives is emotionally charged, the best presentation of "facts" can often have the opposite effect; it can cause the other person to become even more entrenched in their perspective and be more resistant to change. Humans are not very rational in many ways, and when one tries to advocate for their perspective, others often feel their perspectives are being discredited as being "wrong." To reach someone who has a different perspective requires us to set aside our own views for a moment and attempt to understand theirs.

It's difficult to see others' perspectives, but it is a necessary condition for change to take place. Whether we're trying to change others' perspective on which beverage is the best or which support will actually benefit autistic people, if we charge in with a single perspective as being the absolute truth in contradiction to all other perspectives we're trying to change, I guarantee two things will happen:

1. Perspectives won't change.

2. Problems will result.

Change involves a huge emotional component, and if we do not appeal to the human desire to be heard and understood, our efforts will fail. Instead of presenting facts or asserting your perspective as the correct one, the more powerful approach is to listen. Ask about the perspectives of those you are trying to convince to change. Find out why they believe what they believe, assume what they assume, do what they do, and value what they value. In doing so, you create a space where implicit worldviews, which are responsible for the perspective, are made explicit. This allows everyone involved to dig deeper into the reasons why people hold certain perspectives. If one were to take this approach, I guarantee these three things will happen:

1. People will be more comfortable to share.

2. Trust between people will be built.

3. Minds will be opened to other perspectives.

By validating one's perspective, we satisfy some of human's most basic and psychological needs. It's when these needs are met that we can examine our values, beliefs, and assumptions, question what is right and wrong, explore alternatives, and create change. In the process of asking questions to understand others' perspectives, we have the opportunity to check our own assumptions, explore our own worldview in relation to others' worldviews, and consider alternative perspectives for ourselves. Eventually, if we engage in this true dialogue, we will have the chance to share our perspectives with others and possibly even create a completely new reality.

But Don't I Have to Give Up My Perspective?

Asking about others' perspectives doesn't mean you give up your perspectives. While one has to be vulnerable to explore another's perspective, your perspective is still your own and it won't change unless you decide it should change. Any change in your perspective is the result of expanding your worldview and weighing any available evidence in the process. Just like *you* cannot direct a change in *others'* perspectives, *they* cannot direct a change in *your* perspectives merely by an exchange of words.

Perspectives evolve over time—they all do. Perspectives are never absolutely fixed, as we continually have life experiences that directly or indirectly influence our worldview. With every new experience, whether conscious or unconscious, we are perpetually adjusting our worldview.

A Parting Thought on My Perspective

I have been an educator for almost 30 years. As part of my education in how people learn, I was exposed to and studied in depth many different teaching philosophies. During this time, in conjunction with my own teaching practice, I learned about behaviorism and evolved my perspective on why I do not like this approach to teaching and learning.

Since being formally identified as autistic and learning about the autistic community, I learned about applied behavioral analysis (ABA). At first, I thought, "Well, it's not ALL bad. Parents and ABA practitioners only want to ensure children will be successful in life." I opened myself up to learning both sides of the ABA debate, listened to a wide variety of people and perspectives, and read countless studies, books, and the like. Over time, my perspective changed and I began to speak out on this and other issues with which the autistic community contends. I also separated ABA from the ABA practitioners and realized that the people aren't the problem, it is the foundational philosophy, behaviorism, and its primary modus operandi, operant conditioning, that are problematic. Once we can separate these two and explore them separately for what and who they are, we can more objectively see the problems and identify appropriate solutions.

As I began advocating, my advocacy approach was largely unilateral—here is *my* perspective and *you* need to listen to *me*. In having this approach, I started to see what many in the autistic community called "infighting." Different autistic people were asserting their perspectives as the only valid perspective... and I was one of them. I started examining what I asserted and saw how narrow my focus was on *my* lived experience. I started hearing when other autistic people and their loved ones said things like, "But you're not like X because you can..." They were right. I didn't understand others' perspectives, despite having common experiences with them. That is when I leaned on my change management background and decided to change my own perspective. What did I do? It was quite simple... I:

1. Stopped using a "Here is what you need to hear about my autistic experience" platform

2. Started asking about others' perspectives and experiences, especially those who had different perspectives from my own

With this approach, I quickly began to see arguments change to conversations. Those with whom I engaged began to grow in number and new insights into perspectives were revealed. I learned that despite all my studying I did *not* know everything I needed to know. I developed more relationships with people based on commonalities, even with those who supported that which I opposed. Trust became the single greatest influence steering conversations. People began to seek out my counsel regarding their challenges (which I remain honored!) and started sharing my questions to propagate the dialogue. I witnessed perspectives change—not because of coercion, but because of reflection.

To me, *this* is what advocacy is all about: bringing together people from different backgrounds to talk about key issues that affect the marginalized (and indirectly, everyone else) in a productive way by first seeking to understand, *then* seeking to be understood. If advocates only give information and never receive information, we'll stay in a perpetual cycle of doing what we've always done and there will be winners and losers. Advocacy is a two-way street.

Chapter 9
A Relational Model to Understand Neurodiversity

"It is time for parents to teach your people early on that in diversity, there is beauty, and there is strength."

~ Maya Angelou

In a world of infinitely possible human experiences, does it make sense to categorize and pathologize some neurotypes? Does differentiating autistic, ADHD, or dyslexic people from one another, assuming supports are available for all as they need and want them? These are things that I ponder as I continue on my journey of autistic discovery. The further I travel and the more experiences I have, the more I refine my perspectives. Currently, I am on the precipice of deciding that autism doesn't even really exist as we believe it to exist today. It's becoming increasingly difficult to accept that autistic people are somehow differently unique from the uniqueness across all humanity. Put another way, what makes my difference different from everyone else's difference? Instead of focusing on difference, I take a different look at neurodiversity—the commonalities—to explore an alternative explanation for our experiences, which will stay consistent across all individuals.

All too often, autism is associated with some bell-curve visual representation. In this representation, the vertical axis denotes the number of people and the horizontal axis represents some construct of differing neurology. Unfortunately, the horizontal axis often depicts constructs like IQ[60], ability, or functioning, which are inherently ableist and contribute to perpetuating stereotypes about autism; however, this model is rife with problems. For example, the constructs are frequently vaguely defined and don't account for the diversity of experiences within the autistic community. What does it mean to have "typical" functioning, and who decides what is "typical?" The resulting bell curve model thus paints a broad and generalized picture of the autism community that often fails to accurately represent the variety of individual experiences. These constructs also don't hold across contexts and ignore the reality that every person's experiences can shift according to their environment and situation. Consequently, the result is a visual depiction of people that is fundamentally skewed and far from representative of the true diversity and complexity within the autistic community.

I've been guilty of using the same bell curve graph to communicate something about autism myself, but the more I learned about autism by engaging other autistics and non-autistics to understand their perspectives, I began to question the validity of this model. The more I critically reflected on my worldview with others' perspectives, the less sense the bell curve model made to me. Eventually, I came to understand that there are basic commonalities across humanity that could be expressed in three broad domains: internal experiences, external experiences, and support needs for survival.

Three Common Human Experiences

The first common human experience is the infinite range of possible interaction experiences people can have with the environment; the world outside

---

[60] IQ: Intelligence quotient. A number used to express the apparent relative intelligence of a person. Often a score determined by one's performance on a standardized intelligence test relative to the average performance of others of the same age.

ourselves. As humans, we interact with our environment every moment of our existence. We interact with people, things, and every possible sensory-stimulating aspect of the world in which we live. For instance, the act of walking through a forest involves interacting with rustling leaves, chirping birds, the rugged terrain underfoot, and the scent of the pine trees. This experience is not merely the physical act of walking but also involves a complex interplay of sensory inputs. Every human, in their unique way, will perceive these sensory stimuli differently. Some may find the bird's chirping soothing, while others might be overwhelmed by the cacophony. Thus, these external experiences shape our lives and our understanding of the world in profound ways. We also experience things directly or indirectly. Unless we are in a complete vacuum, completely deprived of any stimulus, we all have external experiences. These external experiences help to shape who we are and our lives in profound ways. These experiences can be felt by one person or many people simultaneously at any point in time, though the experience may differ person to person.

The second common human experience is the infinite range of possible sensory experiences individuals can have within themselves. This set of experiences differs from the first common human experience in that only the individual can experience them. These experiences do not exist outside the individual's body, making the experiences absolutely unique to the individual. Such experiences can include emotions, thoughts, sensations, movements, or the like. They can be in response to an external stimulus, but are never the external stimuli itself. These experiences can only be felt by the individual. While the individual can articulate their experience with others, it can never be directly experienced by anyone but the individual. To illustrate, imagine eating a slice of your favorite pie. The taste, the texture, and the aroma are sensory experiences that are incredibly personal and unique to you. Beyond just taste, you might also experience a flood of emotions or memories associated with the pie—perhaps it was a staple at family gatherings or a treat you rewarded yourself with after achieving a goal. This swirl of internal experiences—emotions, thoughts, sensations—can only be truly known by the individual, even though they can be described to others.

Finally, the third common human experience is the infinite range of survival experiences every human has as social beings. These experiences are what help us survive in this world and take an infinite number of forms. At a basic level, these survival experiences include those things that enable us to live and grow from birth (and before), such as food, water, shelter, and clothing. They can also include a sense of love, belonging, and money, to name a few. In the context of disabilities, these support needs include any sort of help by others to enable daily living, communication, or adjustments to reduce stress. In short, this range of human experience includes the survival interactions we have with others to help us make it to the next moment in time and beyond. At the most fundamental level, we need food and water. But beyond that, we also need things like social interaction and a sense of belonging. Consider a child learning to read; they require support from adults, educational materials, and an encouraging environment to succeed. This extends to other individuals who may require different types of support to navigate daily life, like assistive technology for communication or physical adjustments to minimize environmental stress. These survival experiences are diverse, spanning basic needs to complex social interactions, and are crucial to our existence.

Thinking About Neurodiversity as a Relationship

I developed this theoretical model to represent the experiences of every human as a relationship of all possible human experiences, which makes this a more accurate depiction of autism than the more commonly referred bell curve model. In this model, the X axis represents all possible external experiences, the Y axis represents all possible internal experiences, and the Z axis represents all possible survival experiences. This conceptualization also aligns with Spielman, Jenkins, and

Lovett's[61] definition of consciousness, "which describes our awareness of internal and external stimuli. Awareness of internal stimuli includes feeling pain, hunger, thirst, sleepiness, and being aware of our thoughts and emotions. Awareness of external stimuli includes experiences such as seeing the light from the sun, feeling the warmth of a room, and hearing the voice of a friend." What's more, this model is inclusive of *all* humans, not just a subset, which aligns with the neurodiversity paradigm. According to Singer[62], neurodiversity is "a biological truism that refers to the limitless variability of human nervous systems on the planet, in which no two can ever be exactly alike due to the influence of environmental factors."

Each point in the 3-dimensional scatterplot represents an individual's total experience *at a given point in time*. This total experience is the combination of internal, external, and survival experiences, which are contextually bound and perpetually dynamic. A change in any of the three experience domains can affect where in the scatterplot one exists, which can be the same location as another, a slightly different location, or a vastly different location. The relative location one is at any given time is both the result of experience interactions as well as an indication of what sort of experiences they need for survival. Over time, each individual develops a zone they occupy in different general contexts, such as when they are happy, stressed, or productive.

Assuming that each person, regardless of neurotype (as currently defined by various social constructs), has varying internal experiences, external experiences, and survival experiences, and these experiences are dynamic (they perpetually fluctuate), the cluster we see in the center of this snapshot of time will perpetually change in terms of its location, density, and characteristics. This is a better approximation of reality and provides a better, holistic explanation for the vast array of experience differences within the autistic community and the rest of humanity.

---

[61] Spielman, R. M., Jenkins, W. J., & Lovett, M. D. (2020). *Psychology* (2nd Ed.). OpenStax.
[62] Singer, J. (2023). *Reflections on neurodiversity*. https://neurodiversity2.blogspot.com/p/what.html

A Relational Model to Understand Neurodiversity

Frasard Experience Model

∞

Survival Experiences

∞

Internal Experiences

External Experiences

Dr. Scott Frasard © 2023

∞

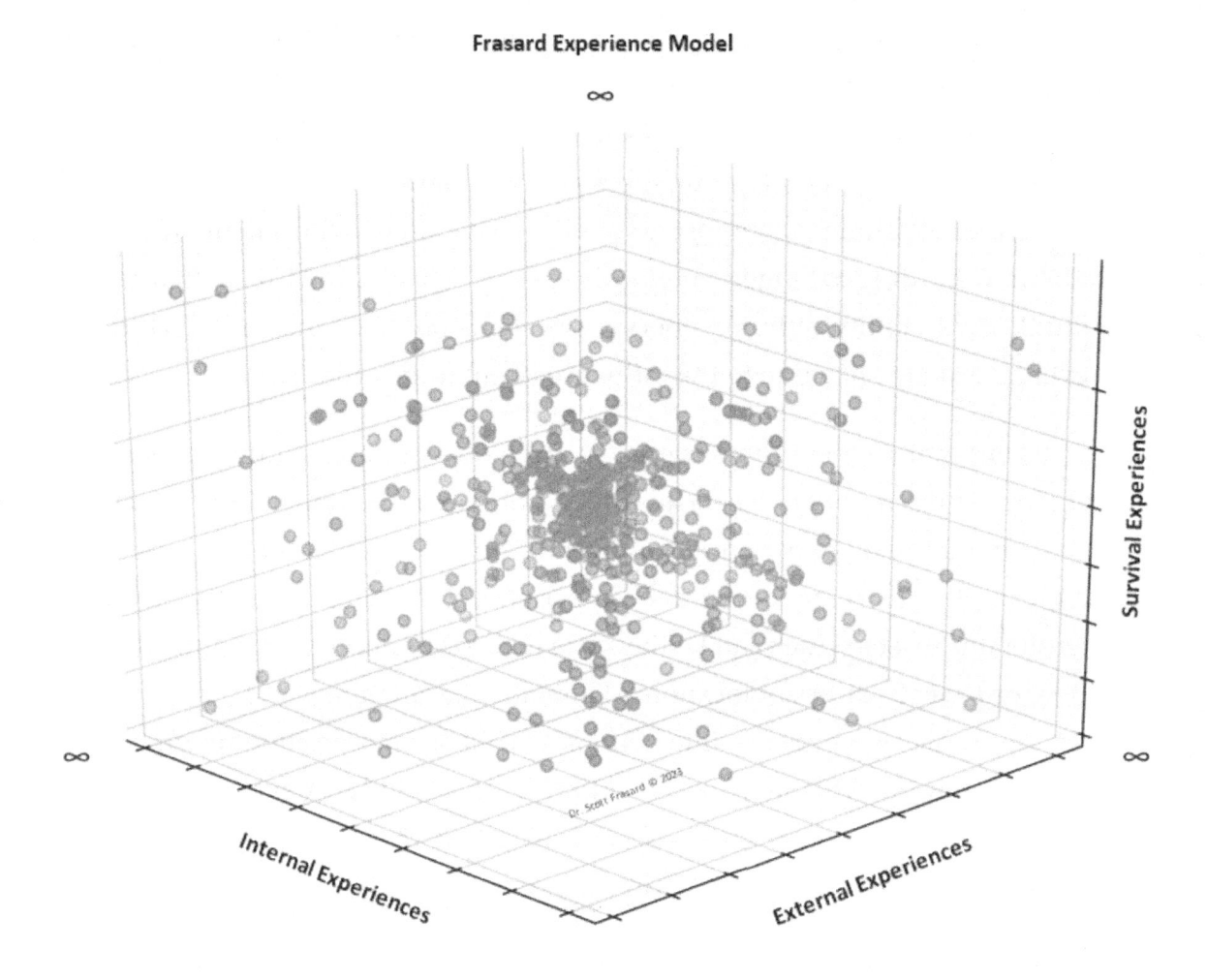

If we accept the premises described above, it is not possible to have a constant "typical" experience and thus, "neurotypical" could not exist. By extension, if neurotypical does not exist, then neurodivergent also does not exist—at least not in a static state. People of any neurotype can have similar experiences with any others, but land in a different location in this scatterplot, despite being categorized as the same neurotype. Through this lens, I sincerely question whether or not neurodivergence actually exists. There may be some logic behind the idea that "we're all autistic," while simultaneously being a patently false claim. Perhaps we are all experientially different.

Consider what would happen if we conceptualized human experiences through a dynamic, three-dimensional lens, one that would allow us to abandon the restrictive concept of neurotypes altogether. This concept would mean a shift from static labels to a more fluid, continuously evolving understanding of human cognition and behavior. The idea here is not to obliterate the understanding of the varied ways in which the brain functions, but rather to refine our understanding of these variations, offering a broader, more inclusive perspective.

Under such a dynamic construct, we could redesign how support is provided and completely eliminate the need for individuals to "qualify" for support based on predefined categories. Instead, we could focus on creating better, more relevant survival experiences for all people. This idea is rooted in understanding that people need different forms and levels of support at different times, regardless of what labels we attach to the infinite combinations of their internal and external experiences. This reconceptualization also enhances our understanding of how our actions, the environment, and the individual's experiences collectively contribute to either promoting a better life for someone or exacerbating their challenges. It could prompt us to acknowledge the vast array of possible experiences, accommodating for their complex interplay, and adjusting our actions accordingly. It may seem like a bold aspiration, but it's not impossible if we dare to dream!

Let's now delve into some of the reasons why eliminating the concept of neurotypes might be beneficial, and how this model could potentially address them. First, removing neurotype labels would play a significant role in reducing stigma and stereotyping. Society often forms biases based on these labels, viewing and treating individuals through the lens of their assigned neurotype rather than their unique personhood, which are often entrenched in the medical/deficit model. By eliminating these labels, we might cultivate a societal mindset that values individuality and diversity without prejudice, acknowledging the shared human experience while still honoring the uniqueness of every person.

A second advantage of abandoning the concept of neurotypes would pave the way for more inclusive practices, particularly in crucial areas such as education and employment. In an ideal world, our systems would be designed to be accessible to everyone from the outset, rather than being primarily tailored for a "neurotypical" majority, with adjustments made as an afterthought for those who are considered "neurodivergent." This means educational curricula that cater to all learners, employment environments that value different types of cognitive strengths, and societal infrastructures that universally consider the diversity of human experiences. The goal would be to foster a culture of acceptance and support, rather than alienation and marginalization. It's about shifting our thinking to understand that the variety in our experiences is not only normal, but a vital part of what makes us human and can lead to innovative problem-solving and a more comprehensive perspective on the world.

A third advantage of abandoning the concept of neurotypes would be an increased emphasis on understanding individuals' experiences rather than assigning them to specific categories. Identifying specific neurotypes is largely subjective, prone to error, and can potentially restrict an individual's potential. By focusing on the dynamic range of human experiences, we can promote empathy, connection, and a more nuanced understanding of the diverse ways we interact with the world. Additionally, this approach can help reduce stigma associated with specific labels, encouraging a culture that is more accepting and inclusive. By valuing the individual's unique experiences and perceptions, we could also encourage a more personalized approach in fields such as therapy, education, and healthcare, which often rely heavily on generalizations based on neurotype classifications. Furthermore, understanding experiences in the context of the whole person may lead to more accurate support and interventions, thereby improving outcomes and overall quality of life.

A fourth advantage of abandoning the concept of neurotypes would be the provision of support tailored to individual needs rather than generic labels. We could design personalized support mechanisms to facilitate a better life experience for individuals, closely aligned with their unique circumstances and ever-evolving needs. Moreover, in the healthcare setting, treatment plans could be designed to be more responsive and adaptive to a patient's unique experience and progression, rather than a one-size-fits-all approach often associated with a specific neurotype. Additionally, in the workplace, employers could better foster an inclusive environment by creating personalized strategies that boost the productivity and wellbeing of each employee, rather than providing general adjustments that may not be as effective for every individual. This approach would likely lead to more equitable opportunities, increased satisfaction, and overall improved outcomes in various life domains.

A fifth advantage of abandoning the concept of neurotypes would encourage a broader view of human diversity. By eliminating neurotype labels, we would foster greater acceptance and understanding among individuals, acknowledging the fluid and infinite possible human experiences. In a society where neurotypes are not seen as rigid, defining characteristics, we can promote a more inclusive, accepting worldview where every person's uniqueness is not just tolerated, but celebrated. This perspective shift can lead to healthier interpersonal dynamics, as people would be less likely to make judgments based on predefined categories, and instead, appreciate others' unique life experiences and perspectives. Moreover, this could also play a pivotal role in mitigating stigma associated with certain neurotypes, leading to enhanced social inclusion and acceptance for individuals who may currently face negative stereotypes or discrimination. Ultimately, such an approach reinforces the premise that our neurological variations are part of what makes us human, and that this inherent diversity enriches our shared human experience.

Finally, a sixth advantage of abandoning the concept of neurotypes would force an emphasis on the dynamic nature of human experiences, rather than static labels, which will promote continuous learning and adaptation. It could be more reflective of the human condition, where growth, change, and the capacity to adapt are intrinsic aspects of our journey. This new approach could shift our mindset towards embracing the complexities of the human mind, fostering a deeper, more enriched understanding of ourselves and others. With this dynamic perspective, we can recognize and validate that our internal and external experiences and support needs can vary significantly across different situations and periods in our life, instead of being confined to a singular, unchanging neurotype. It will also encourage a culture of lifelong learning where we continually seek to understand our ever-evolving self and the diversity around us. Finally, we could be better equipped to handle change and adapt to different situations, fostering a more empowered sense of self and the world around us.

In light of these considerations, shifting away from a model centered around neurotypes and towards a more dynamic, relational understanding of human experiences can offer multiple benefits. The potential advantages span from reducing stigma and embracing diversity, to fostering more inclusive and tailored support mechanisms, and encouraging a culture of continuous learning and adaptation. By doing so, we not only pave the way for a more inclusive, understanding, and empathetic society, but also unleash the potential for innovative problem-solving, personal growth, and societal advancement. Such a dynamic, all-encompassing model respects and values the complexity and fluidity of the human mind and its experiences. It may not be an easy journey, and the shift may face resistance, but the promise it holds for creating a more inclusive, supportive, and empathetic society is worth every step. We must keep daring to dream, for it's only in dreaming that we can envision the potential for change and aspire to create a world that acknowledges, appreciates, and celebrates the rich tapestry of human experiences.

Chapter 10
Rethinking Support, Disability, and Advocacy

"At the end of the day, the narratives, myths, and frameworks you use to make sense of the world are only approximations, they are never the truth. If you are able to pick the most suitable one for the moment or your situation, by reframing, this is an essential skill for survival in a fast changing and uncertain world."

~Bryan Callen

I post a lot about autistic support needs. It has generated wonderful conversations about how to support autistic people and even some spirited debate about support needs in general. One thing that has become blatantly obvious to me is that we speak about support needs, we do so with generalities. After speaking with many people, reading many books, articles, and online references, I've found an overwhelming lack of specificity when people try to articulate what "support" really means. To some, it may mean intensive therapies while to others it may mean a simple adjustment in how we think about something (and everything in between). While some specifics are offered, I've yet to come across a comprehensive set for any specific individual.

What's the Big Deal?

I believe the lack of specificity about what support needs mean is a key change component we need to address in order to move towards a positive, productive dialogue about autism outside of the medical/deficit model. Leaving things poorly-defined provides opportunity to broadly interpret meaning and end up not providing meaningful support to those in need. Unless a true open dialogue takes place about these broad interpretations, conflict will result. When I look at the support narrative at large, I see conflict, often in the form of, "But you're not like our autistic child." or "Our child needs soooo much help." While these may be completely accurate in their individual contexts, they don't communicate with sufficient clarity to contribute key support differences to the larger narrative needed, but it doesn't have to be this way.

What Can We Do?

I started thinking about my own support needs. This led me to wonder whether or not people can specify support needs in a meaningful way and if so, can we also quantify support needs? Being able to speak in specifics will make the social model of disability the absolute clear choice for conceptualizing not only autism, but all contexts in which disability results. I believe we can do this!

I took some time to reflect through my days and needed supports. I reflected on a variety of days where I need almost no support and days where I need many supports. I thought about what I ask others to do to help me and what my wife automatically does to help me (the latter being the majority!). I started writing a list of those things and I had an ah-ha! moment. If I take the time, I *can* make explicit the tacit. I *can* precisely articulate my support needs in a way that others can understand. Here is a list of my specific support needs (thus far):

- Time and space to recharge before/after social engagements
- Time and space for me to engage in my routines
- Time and space for me to ask for clarification about messages/instructions

- Time and space for me to info dump
- Time and space for me to process information
- Time and space for me to address problematic sensory issues
- Time and space for me to answer your questions to completeness as I define it
- Scheduling appointments for me
- Accompany me to appointments as needed
- Intervening/speaking on my behalf when I'm struggling to or cannot communicate
- Technology troubleshooting
- Making some decisions for me
- Answering my exact question when asked
- Allowing me to stim
- Providing short, succinct, and sometimes written instructions
- Being direct
- Going to a different public place (e.g., restaurants) if the selected one is too loud/crowded
- Earplugs when I am in unavoidably loud places
- Adjusting recipes to meet my limited palate
- Reducing the temperature at night so I can sleep
- A room free of any light at night so I can sleep

With this reflection activity, I both specified and quantified my support needs (n=21, currently). What's more, I have something tangible I can share with my friends, family, employer, colleagues, etc. when I want to communicate my needs or when they ask how they can help. Lastly, none of these are unreasonable for anyone, which makes support easy to provide.

The main point is that we can and should stop talking about support needs in generalities. Being ambiguous is not very helpful and causes confusion and/or conflict. We can finally move away from damaging functioning labels to something that provides others with the specificity needed to actually help, especially in times of crisis. Doing so also honors the unique and dynamic nature of support needs each person has, not just autistic people—*all* people!

Typical Thinking About Autism Disability and Support Needs

When we think about autism and disability, we might envision a range of possible abilities. As noted previously, this may conjure up the image of a normal distribution curve[63] where those who are not autistic are on one end (the left) and those who are autistic on the other end. This range of people (and the frequencies) are represented in a way to organize them based on the challenges they face or how productive they are – also known as how well they "function."

This way of thinking is problematic for a number of reasons, but there are two primary reasons that come to my mind. First, "functionality" is a dynamic interaction between the person and their environment. Second, value is attached to how much or well one functions. In a capitalistic society, those who are "low-functioning" are often perceived as less valuable or worthy because of some production ability while those who are "high-functioning" are more valuable or worthy. This thinking neglects the intrinsic value of people and reduces the human experience to a resource that is meant to be exploited for profit. This strips autistic people of agency, ignoring the talents possessed by the former while downplaying the struggles faced by the latter, which is among the many reasons a large portion of autistic people dislike functioning labels.

---

[63] Sabariego, C., Oberhauser, C., Posarac, A., Bickenback, J., Kosanjsek, N., Chatterji, S., Officer, A., Coenen, M., Chhan, L., & Cieza, A. (2015). Measuring disability: Comparing the impact of two data collection approaches on disability rates. *International Journal of Environmental Research and Public Health, 13*(1), 10329-10351. doi: 10.3390/ijerph120910329

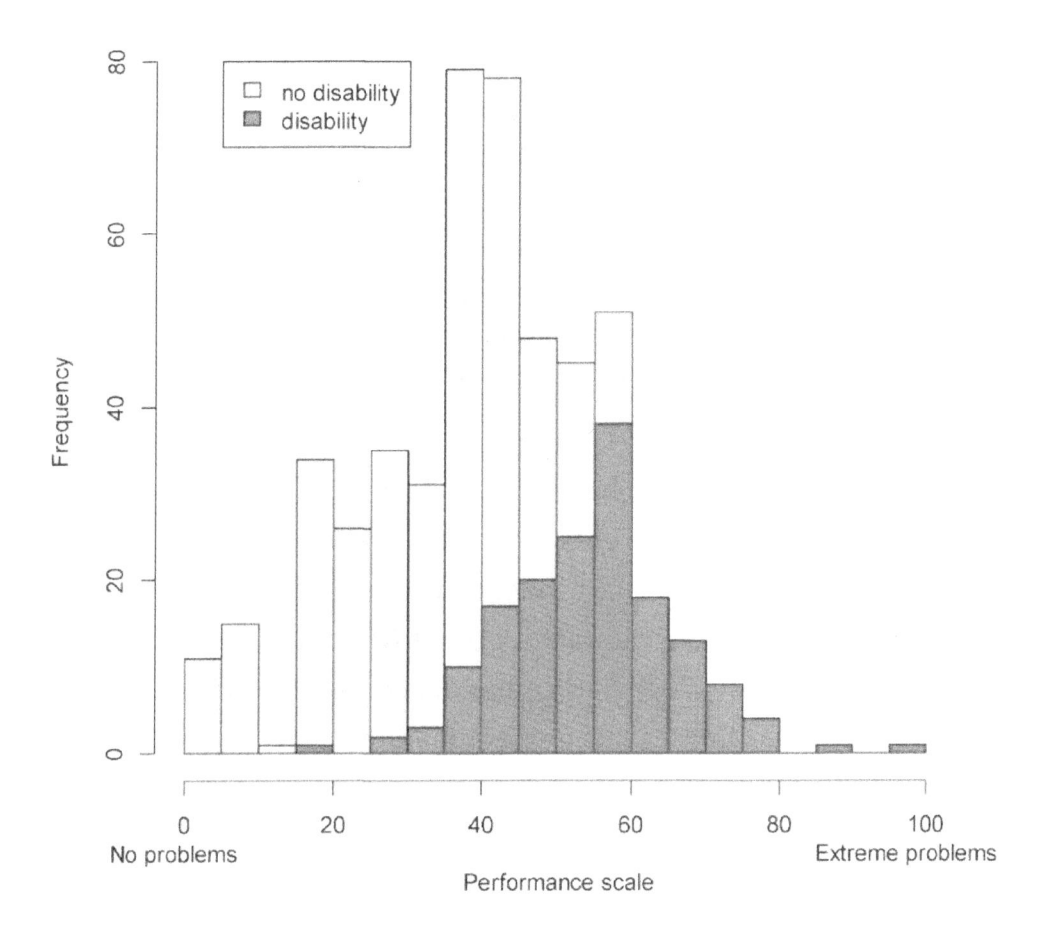

Reframing Support Needs

In the previous chapter, I described how I currently see things as the relationships among three primary common experiences. Turning now to the way we could envision supports, I see people in terms of how much support they need to have meaningful life experiences. These support needs include any imaginable experience to help create more meaningful life for autistic people in their environment. These supports help to better align the mismatches that exist among all possible internal and external experiences. Instead of these support needs being represented as a normal distribution curve as described above, I see them as a log-normal distribution representing the number of people requiring supports, but not attaching any sort of value to that person as a function of their support needs. I also see it as a dynamic state where people transition among various support needs on a continuous basis.

To explain what a log-normal distribution is in simple terms, think about the heights of people. Most people are around the same height, and very few people are really short or really tall. If we made a graph of this, it would look like a bell -- this is what we call a "normal" distribution. Now, consider wealth. Most people don't have much money, a few people have a lot, and there's no limit to how much money a person can have. If we make a graph of this, it doesn't look like a bell, but instead like a slide on a playground. It starts high on the left (most people with less money) and slides down towards the right (few people with lots of money). This is a "log-normal" distribution. The "log" part comes in because if we do a special math trick called taking the "logarithm" of the money amounts, then the graph would look like a bell again. So it's called "log-normal." Lots of things in real life follow this pattern, like wealth, the size of cities, and the lengths of comments on the internet.

The graph below shows the relative proportion of the population along the vertical axis and the relative amount of support individuals need at any given point in time along the horizontal axis. The horizontal axis is organized into five zones of support need categories. These categories are not mutually exclusive and can overlap, which honors the dynamic nature of autistic people's support needs at any given time. Additionally, transitioning from one zone to another does not require any sort of incremental increase/decrease (e.g., Zone A to B to C); quantum transitions (e.g., Zone A to E) can occur.

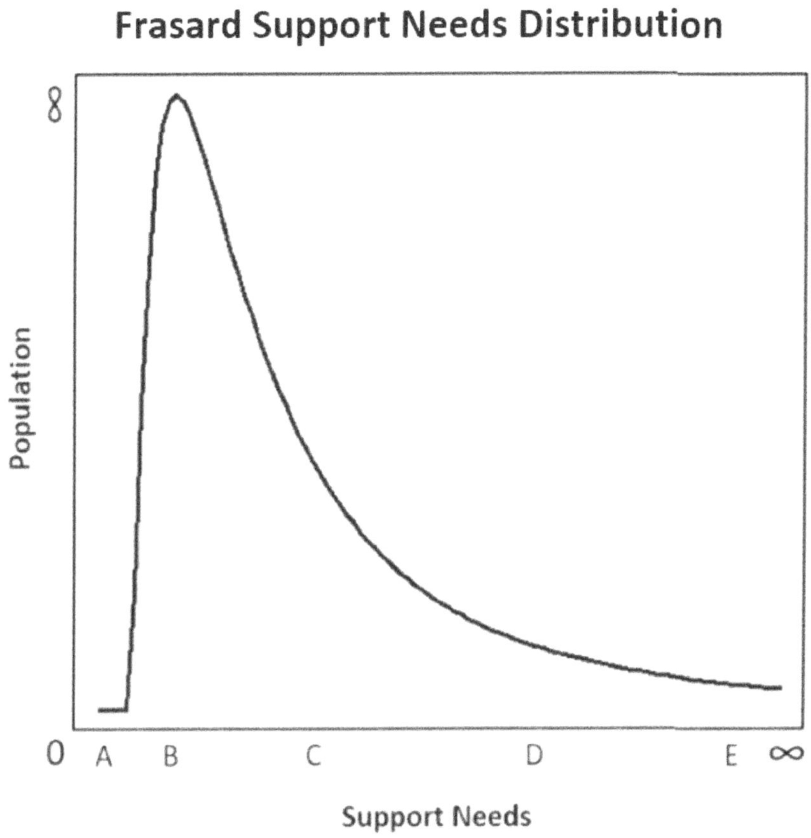
Frasard Support Needs Distribution
∞
Population
0
A
B
C
D
E
∞
Support Needs

Support Zones

People in Zone A require almost no support from anybody or anything else to live a meaningful life and have all sustaining needs met. Unless one is 100% self-sufficient and has no interactions with others, people will have some form of support needs for daily living. This would be an extreme situation, but theoretically not impossible. More likely, this is a brief moment in time and may be better conceptualized as when one has their support needs satisfied but before the next support need arises.

People in Zone B require some support needs, but these are minimal in frequency, amount, scope, and/or purpose. These needs arise from interacting with others in daily life and are associated mostly with interpersonal engagement (e.g., "social norms") and life-sustaining needs (e.g., nourishment, clothing, and shelter). Most non-autistic people would be in Zone B most of the time, but may have times when they need more support for a variety of reasons. There is a generalized lack of support needs for this majority because the social interactive world is defined by their experiences and/or their ability to cope with experiences. In other words, the lack of support needs is because the world is designed to automatically support their needs because most people have the same (or very closely similar) support needs.

People in Zone C require more support than those in Zones A and B, which can be highly variable in terms of frequency, amount, scope, and/or purpose. These people may align with what is currently conceptualized as the neuromajority population, may be autistic or non-autistic, and/or may have simultaneously existing medical and/or psychological contexts present. People in Zone C may require some supports to better interact with the neurotypical/neuromajority population on the basis of desire and/or need. These people may also have less internalized trauma as a result of social interactions and/or ability to cope with experiences than people in Zones D or E.

People in Zone D require more support than those in Zones A and B and are less variant than those in Zone C in terms of frequency, amount, scope, and/or purpose. These are people who mostly do not align with what is currently conceptualized as the neuromajority population, are most often autistic, and frequently have simultaneously existing medical and/or neurodevelopmental contexts present. These people often require more supports to better interact with the neurotypical/neuromajority population or for self-care, which may include life-sustaining measures.

People in Zone E are among the most vulnerable autistic people. They almost always have simultaneously existing medical and/or neurodevelopmental contexts present, which makes human interaction challenging. Supports are typically persistent and oriented more towards life-sustaining measures than social interaction measures but may include both. People in Zone E often don't or have extreme difficulty transitioning to other Zones of support. Unfortunately, people in Zone E are often written off as something "less" in the human experience, given that they are completely dependent upon others for their survival experiences.

Paradigm Shift

I have spent the last three years since my formal identification as being autistic learning about myself and the autistic community. Many things I once knew as "fact" about autism were actually inaccurate at best and harmful at worst. Among these things is the idea that autistic people range along a continuum of functionality and this continuum is somehow supposed to be useful in some way. The more I read and the more I listen to other autistic people and reflect on my own life experiences, the more I've come to learn this is a very problematic mental model. We need to rethink the idea that autism is an individual disability whereby the problem exists within the person themselves. We need a paradigm shift and see autism as a natural variation in the human neurological existence whereby people are largely disabled by their environment.

Individual Problem ⟷ **Societal Support**

In order to truly help autistic people we need to accept that society must do the majority of the change to provide support that helps align mismatched human interactions. This is not to say that non-autistics must bow before autistics and cater to their every whim. Rather, this is a shift to a universal design mental model whereby what enables an autistic person to thrive also enables the neuromajority to thrive. We need to abandon the idea that autistic people can be "taught" to be more like non-autistic people or to fit some socially acceptable way of behaving. We need to stop conceptualizing autism as a collection of deficits that are meant to be corrected. We need to stop self-fulfilling prophecies that relegate autistic people to some lesser version of existence.

As a start, I challenge everyone who reads this to compile their own list of support needs. Take the time to clearly articulate what is vague as *you* are the ultimate beneficiary. If you're like me, you could take it to the next level and use that to measure support needs in a variety of ways such as frequency, timing, duration, or perhaps factors associated with needing support and results of those supports to better understand when, why, and how these supports help. Perhaps on a large-scale, such an understanding would reveal ways people from all walks of life can create a better environment for all, but especially for autistic people.

Afterward

As we reach the end of this book, we arrive at a new beginning. This particular journey has been a personal odyssey, a voyage that began with the revelation at age 48 that I am autistic, where I explored my own identity, self-acceptance, and advocacy. This book, and the 1,226 questions it raises, represents far more than a personal journey—it is a beacon of hope and a call to action for the millions who share this autistic identity with me.

Writing this book was more than an intellectual pursuit; it was a cathartic exploration into the heart of my own experience and those of countless others in the autistic community. It has been a year of introspection, of painstaking inquiry, of relentless advocacy, and of persistent hope. It is the culmination of personal reflection, of learning from others, and of channeling the strength and courage to confront an often-misunderstood reality. To the autistic and adjacent communities, my heartfelt gratitude is boundless. I owe so much to your wisdom, your experiences, and your voices. Your resilience has been my inspiration; your stories have become the lifelines that weave this narrative. Together, we represent a wide range of experiences, a diversity of perspectives, and yet, we share a common bond—we are all human!

It is my conviction that all perspectives are valid and valuable and that each narrative contributes to our understanding of autism's vastness. We do not live in a world of black and white; rather, our world is painted in a kaleidoscope of colors, each perspective adding another valuable hue. Sharing differing experiences creates a richer tapestry of insight, which deepens our collective understanding of what it truly means to be autistic. The power of empathy in bridging our differences cannot be overstated, for in acknowledging and respecting our diverse viewpoints, we foster a community that is not only inclusive but also compassionate and empathetic. What's more, disagreement should not be seen as a cause for division, but as an opportunity for growth in understanding. Every divergence is a chance to expand our horizons, to learn, to challenge our preconceptions, and to stamp out misunderstandings. It is the friction of these conflicting views that can ignite the sparks of enlightenment. Hence, embracing such variance is not a burden but a privilege.

I invite you to consider even those viewpoints that diverge from your own, as they are the sparks that ignite conversations and will lead to meaningful and sustainable change. With open hearts and minds, we must step beyond the comfortable realms of our personal perspectives and venture into the broader landscape of collective experience. In this shared space of understanding and discourse, transformative change takes root.

If there is one overarching theme to this work, it is the need to critically examine what we know (or believe we know) about autism and autistic people. We must challenge and question our existing beliefs about autism, examining them through the prism of lived experience, and incorporate scientific understanding. This journey is not only about gaining new insights but also about discarding old stereotypes and misperceptions.

As an autistic author, my passion is to uplift and amplify the voices of all autistic people. This book, in all its chapters, in all its questions, in all its assertions, is a testament to that passion. It is a plea for the world to listen, to understand, and to accept us for who we are. These chapters gave inspiration for my Autistic Bill of Rights, which is more than a mere statement; it is a proclamation of our inherent dignity, a declaration of our innate worth, and a commitment to honor these rights. It is a clarion call for all autistic people to be recognized, respected, and protected. With this book, I hope to ignite a flame of understanding, a beacon of hope, and a pathway to change. This is my sincere contribution to a cause close to my heart and central to my existence. This is a plea for acceptance, for empathy, for a world that listens and understands.

My wish is that these words, this journey, and these questions touch your heart, spark your curiosity, and inspire you to join me in empathetically exploring others' perspectives regarding autism. Because this is not just my story or your story—it is our story. Through sharing our stories, understanding our experiences, and valuing our perspectives that we can bring about real, lasting change. So, as you close this book, may its echoes remain with you. Let's continue the dialogue, let us keep asking questions, let us continue to advocate for all autistic people, for our voices matter, our experiences matter, and our rights matter. Let this be more than just a book. Let it be the beginning of a movement, a call to action, and a bridge towards a world where every autistic individual is recognized, appreciated, and celebrated. Let us imagine—and create—that world together.

Autistic Bill of Rights

In the journey of advocating for myself and the broader autistic community over the past year and a half, I have encountered a diverse range of perspectives and experiences. These interactions have inspired me to articulate the fundamental rights that I believe every autistic person should be guaranteed. The Autistic Bill of Rights is not just a set of principles; it is a declaration of the inherent dignity, worth, and potential of autistic individuals. It is a call to recognize and honor the unique contributions of autistic people, and to ensure that our society provides the acceptance, respect, and support that we deserve. This document represents a commitment to fostering an inclusive world where neurodiversity is celebrated, and every autistic person can thrive. I am proud to present to you my version of an Autistic Bill of Rights.

Autistic Bill of Rights

Preamble: Every person, regardless of neurology, possesses inherent value, potential, and rights. In recognition of the unique experiences and challenges faced by autistic individuals in a world often not designed for them, this Autistic Bill of Rights affirms autistic individuals' rights to acceptance, respect, and support that values their neurodiversity.

1. **Right to Exist:** Autistic people have the unequivocal right to exist as they are, without fear of eradication or forced normalization. Autistic traits and characteristics are integral aspects of their identity and must be accepted and celebrated.

2. **Right to Life and Preservation:** Autistic individuals have the inviolable right to life, survival, and physical safety. This encompasses the right to live in secure, supportive environments, free from threats, violence, or neglect. Their lives must be valued and protected on an equal basis with others, under all circumstances and at all stages of life.

3. **Right to Identity:** Autistic people have the indisputable right to identify as autistic and to view their autism as an integral and valued part of their identity.

4. **Right to Self-Expression:** Autistic individuals have the right to express themselves freely and authentically and to have their unique communication methods acknowledged and respected.

5. **Right to Autonomy and Self-Determination:** Autistic individuals have the right to self-determination, autonomy, and agency over their bodies, minds, and lives. This includes making decisions regarding therapies, medical treatments, and daily living routines.

6. **Right to Accessibility and Accommodation:** Autistic people have the right to accessible environments, services, and tools that respect their sensory, communication, and processing differences. This includes adaptive technology, quiet spaces, and flexibility in educational and professional settings.

7. **Right to Social Inclusion:** Autistic people have the right to full and active participation in community activities, social discourse, and all aspects of societal life. They should be provided the necessary support and accommodations to actively participate and have their voices heard.

8. **Right to Communication:** Autistic individuals have the right to communicate in their preferred manner, be it through speech, sign language, alternative and augmentative communication (AAC) devices, or other forms of expression. Society must strive to understand and value all forms of communication.

9. **Right to Education and Employment:** Autistic people have the right to inclusive, flexible, and supportive educational and work environments that recognize their strengths and accommodate their needs. They should have access to educational and professional opportunities that foster growth and development, leading to meaningful, fulfilling employment.

10. **Right to Freedom from Harm:** Autistic individuals have the right to live free from physical, emotional, and psychological harm, including harmful interventions, restraint, seclusion, or discrimination of any kind.

11. **Right to Healthcare:** Autistic people have the right to comprehensive healthcare that acknowledges and respects their neurodiversity, sensory sensitivities, and communication needs. They should have equitable access to physical and mental health services, with consent and autonomy at the forefront.

12. **Right to Policy Inclusion:** Autistic individuals have the right to be included in public policy decision-making processes, particularly those that directly affect them. Their views and experiences must be genuinely considered and valued in shaping policies that influence their lives.

13. **Right to Advocacy and Representation:** Autistic people have the right to self-advocacy and fair representation in all forums. Autistic voices should lead the discussion on autism, and their experiences should shape policies, practices, and narratives about autism.

14. **Right to Privacy:** Autistic individuals have the right to privacy and confidentiality in all aspects of life. Personal details, including their formal autism identification, should be shared only with explicit consent.

By affirming these rights, we strive towards a more equitable and inclusive society, one in which every autistic individual is respected, valued, and allowed to thrive as their authentic selves. We reject the commoditization of autism and commit to a world that honors and nurtures neurodiversity in all its forms.

About the Author

Dr. Scott Frasard is an experienced learning leader and has worked in government, academic, and corporate organizations in a global context. Scott is an adult educator of 30 years, has an M.Ed. and PhD in Adult Education from The University of Georgia and a M.Ed. in Measurement, Evaluation, Statistics, and Assessment from the University of Illinois – Chicago. He is currently a manager and psychometrician full time in a global tech industry organization, teaches part time at the undergraduate level, speaks at conferences globally on adult education and evaluation topics, and publishes in these areas.

Scott's research agenda focuses on alternative means of evaluating instructor effectiveness and organizational intervention sustainability. At age 48, Scott was formally identified as being autistic. Since then, he has expanded his research agenda to include increasing instructor acceptance of neurodiversity issues in corporate and higher education and evaluating the impact of teaching strategies in the neurodiverse learner population. He is an autism advocate, speaking to a wide audience on various neurodiversity-affirming topics important to the autistic community. In April 2022, Scott launched an advocacy campaign on LinkedIn under the moniker, "A Reflective Question to Ponder" that aimed to foster fruitful dialogue among people with differing perspectives about autism and autistic people in order to better understand the values, beliefs, and assumptions that bring rise to these perspectives.

In 2019, Scott was honored by The University of Georgia's Mary Francis Early College of Education as one of their inaugural inductees of the Circle of 50, in recognition of his important contributions to research and practice in adult education, learning, leadership, and organizational development in the Department of Lifelong Education, Administration, and Policy's 50 years of graduate programs. In 2023, Scott was honored by Neurodiversity World – Powered by Dynamics Group UK as one of the top 50 Neurodiversity Evangelists globally. Scott also authored the Autistic Bill of Rights, which is included at the end of this book.

Made in the USA
Columbia, SC
19 December 2024